Bulimia Nervosa

of related interest

Anorexics on Anorexia
Edited by Rosemary Shelley
ISBN 1 85302 471 6

Figures of Lightness
Anorexia, Bulimia and Psychoanalysis
Gabriella Ripa di Meana
ISBN 1 85302 617 4

More than Just a Meal
The Art of Eating Disorders
Susan R. Makin
ISBN 1 85302 805 3

Self Mutilation and Art Therapy
Violent Creation
Diana Milia
ISBN 1 85302 683 2

Arts Therapies and Clients with Eating Disorders
Fragile Board
Edited by Ditty Dokter
ISBN 1 85302 256 X

Bulimia Nervosa

A Cognitive Therapy Programme for Clients

Myra Cooper, Gillian Todd and Adrian Wells

Jessica Kingsley Publishers
London and Philadelphia

First published in the United Kingdom in 2000 by
Jessica Kingsley Publishers Ltd,
116 Pentonville Road, London
N1 9JB, England
and
325 Chestnut Street,
Philadelphia PA 19106, USA.

www.jkp.com

© Copyright 2000 Myra Cooper, Gillian Todd and Adrian Wells

Library of Congress Cataloging in Publication Data
A CIP catalog record for this book is available from the Library of Congress

British Library Cataloguing in Publication Data
A CIP catalogue record for this book is available from the British Library

ISBN 1 85302 717 0

Printed and Bound in Great Britain by
Athenaeum Press, Gateshead, Tyne and Wear

Contents

Preface

Bulimia nervosa is a distressing and disabling problem. It is becoming very common. If you've picked up this book because you have bulimia nervosa then, like most sufferers, you're probably tired of it ruling your life. You're probably keen, even desperate, to find help to recover. You may have struggled long and hard for some time to overcome the problem by yourself; you may have had little or no success. This book offers you new help as well as new hope. It presents a detailed self-help cognitive therapy programme, designed specifically for bulimia nervosa.

The idea of self-help has become popular in recent years. You are probably familiar with the term; it means learning how to help yourself. However, you are probably less familiar with the term cognitive therapy. Cognitive therapy is a recently developed psychological treatment; it was first devised for depression by Professor A.T. Beck in the USA. Since then it has been applied to many other problems. It focuses particularly on 'cognitions' or thoughts, and on the interrelationship between thoughts, feelings and behaviour. It has only a short history, but it has established itself as a highly effective treatment for many psychological problems, including eating disorders. Unfortunately, it usually involves a course of individual treatment with a skilled therapist. This is an option that, for a variety of reasons, is not readily available to everyone who might find it helpful. This is worrying for people with bulimia nervosa because research shows that it is one of the few therapies that helps people with eating disorders. Recently, however, several cognitive therapy treatments have been turned (very successfully) into self-help programmes and some have been published in book form, making them much more widely available. Cognitive therapy is ideally suited to self-help and these programmes have helped lots of people with a wide range of problems. At any one time, there are many people with bulimia nervosa who do not have access to individual treatment or help of any kind, let alone cognitive therapy. If you have bulimia nervosa, you may be one of those people. There is also a growing number of people with eating disorders who actively prefer a self-help approach. Like them, you might well benefit from our self-help cognitive therapy programme.

The programme we describe in this book draws on our research experience, and on our combined experience of treating people with bulimia nervosa. It presents many of the well-established, basic cognitive therapy principles, knowledge, skills and strategies that our patients have found helpful. It also draws on some of the exciting new advances that we have made in recent years, as a team, in the understanding of bulimia nervosa and its treatment using cognitive therapy. Throughout the book, we will share our specialist bulimia nervosa and cognitive therapy knowledge, skills and ideas with you. We will also share examples of how some of our patients have used the programme. By completing the exercises, and putting into practice the suggestions we make, you will be using 'state of the art' cognitive therapy to work on your eating problem, by yourself, at home.

If you have bulimia nervosa, we hope, after reading the introductory chapters and considering the book carefully, that you will decide to work through the self-help programme. We also hope, as you progress, that the programme and the examples of the success that our patients have had with it will give you the encouragement, help and support that you need to recover.

A note for friends and partners

If you are a friend or partner of someone with bulimia nervosa then you will have seen how destructive and distressing it can be. Your friend or partner has taken a big and brave step if they have decided to try self-help. You can help and support them by reading through this book, encouraging them to try the exercises and being there when it gets tough. You will probably also find the information in the first few chapters particularly helpful in increasing your understanding of the disorder.

A note for therapists

Although designed as a self-help programme, this book can be used very successfully in individual therapy. It may be particularly useful for those with bulimia nervosa who have additional problems (see Chapter 3) and are in need of professional help.

Acknowledgements

We would like to thank all those patients who helped us develop the programme. They have played an important part by trying out the exercises and strategies described. Their feedback has been invaluable in refining the programme. We would like to thank all the patients who kindly read drafts of the manuscript, as well as those who have taken part, over the last few years, in the research studies on which the programme is based.

PART 1

The Facts

CHAPTER I

Background and Basics

In this chapter we provide a basic grounding for the programme and for the book. We also introduce you to the essential basics of the programme. This information is important. Among other topics, it outlines our aims in writing the book, what you can expect from us and what we expect from you (if you want to maximise your chances of success). There is also a note for older women and for men with bulimia nervosa,[1] and a brief discussion of common worries about recovery.

The aims of the book

The aims of our book are simple and straightforward: to provide you with the information and the practical help that will enable you to overcome your eating disorder.

The programme

The programme will draw on a psychological theory – cognitive theory – and a psychological treatment approach – cognitive therapy. The theory will give you an understanding of your eating problem; in particular, it will give you an explanation of what keeps it going and why it might have developed. The treatment programme, based on cognitive therapy principles, will give you the practical help that you will need in order to recover. The theory and the practical help are closely linked: once you understand the reasons for your problem then you will be in a better position to overcome it.

Development of the programme

This book draws heavily on recent developments by leading scientists and expert therapists in cognitive theory and therapy. These developments have been published in scientific journals, and academic books, and presented at international conferences.

---

1   Because the majority of people with eating disorders are female, we will use the female pronoun throughout the book, where appropriate, to refer to those with bulimia nervosa.

Our role

As scientists and clinicians we have played a role in these new developments. This book is based on that new understanding and those new developments.

Our patients' role

All the suggestions and exercises in the programme have been used successfully by our patients. Their feedback has been invaluable; it has led to modifications and to more new ideas.

What you can expect from this book

In this book you will discover what maintains your eating disorder and why it has developed. Most important of all, you will learn how to use cognitive therapy strategies to overcome it. To make this possible, the book will provide a detailed step-by-step, self-help programme. First, it will focus on encouraging yourself to change. Then it will present the model on which the treatment programme is based. Subsequently, it will cover getting control of your eating, how to identify and challenge problematic thoughts, and how to deal with the behaviours that maintain negative thoughts about weight and shape. It will suggest new ways to tackle the problems that you have been dealing with by bingeing, and help you examine your beliefs about eating, weight and shape and about yourself. It will also help you to break the link between dieting and self-worth. Towards the end of the programme, it will concentrate on improving self-worth and preparing for the future. Each chapter builds on the one before, taking one step at a time.

Our experience with the programme

We have been using the programme successfully for some time with the patients we see in our eating disorder clinics. It has helped people who have recently developed an eating problem. It has helped people whose eating problem has a long history, and people whose problem is very severe. It has also helped those who have previously had anorexia nervosa, or who have been underweight for long periods of time. The book contains many examples, taken from our clinical work, of the particular problems our patients have had and how they have been able to overcome them, using the strategies outlined in the book. Encouraged by the success of the programme in our clinics we turned it into a self-help programme (the basis of this book), making it available to all those who, for one reason or another, do not have ready access to professional help or who prefer a self-help approach. Most of our patients have had some help with the programme from a therapist. However, research suggest that in lots of cases this is not necessary. Cognitive therapy is ideally suited to self-help and has helped many people overcome a wide range of problems by themselves, without professional help. We hope you will find our patients' examples useful and that they will encourage you to try the strategies for yourself.

What you will have to do

To stand a good chance of recovering, you will have to commit yourself wholeheartedly to the programme. You will need to set aside time, not only to read the book, but also to put the suggestions into practice and complete the exercises. Simply reading the book is unlikely to make your eating problem disappear. A colleague of ours has noted that you can read a book about skiing, but would you then know what to do at the top of the slope? The same is true here. You will need to work steadily through the book, from start to finish, and make sure that you carry out all the suggestions that are relevant to your particular problems. You must also try to follow the programme right to the end. Our patients sometimes want to stop treatment, because they feel better, before finishing it. However, we strongly discourage this. Stopping prematurely seems to increase the likelihood of relapse. We want you to get better and stay better.

Many people improve quickly, but some people find that progress is slower than they would like. This is particularly likely to happen if you have had the problem for a very long time or if you feel that it has become part of your personality and character. If progress does seem slow, don't despair. It will simply take time and lots of practice. As long as you are continuing to improve, however slowly, you will almost certainly get there in the end.

Older women and men

Bulimia nervosa is particularly common in teenage girls and young women. However, we are seeing an increasing number of older women, and also men, in our eating disorder clinics. In many cases the symptoms and issues involved appear to be similar to those seen in young women. This suggests that our programme might also be suitable for you if you are older or if you are male. Indeed, a small number of older women and men have already benefited from treatment based on our programme. So, if you are older or male we are optimistic about the programme's ability to help you too.

A word for the worried and the ambivalent

If you have bulimia nervosa then you may well be worried that you will never get better. You may already have tried (and failed) with one or more self-help programmes. You may also be feeling ambivalent about change, and wondering whether it will all be worth it. If you don't have these worries, and you've already decided to commit yourself to the programme, that's very good news. However, it is much more likely that you are feeling pessimistic about recovery and worried that change might just make things worse. In particular, you may be terrified at the thought of having to cope differently with the problems that you are currently dealing with by bingeing. You may be surprised to hear that most of our patients initially have these worries too, and that many of them feel very ambivalent about change. At the very least, it is likely that recovery will mean that you have to make some adjustments to your life. In some cases, recovery might involve more widespread change, as old problems re-emerge and need to be dealt with without bingeing. Nevertheless, people do get better, and it is possible to change and be glad you've changed.

Our patients continually tell us that it really is worth all that effort and commitment. Moreover, recovery is rarely as traumatic or as difficult to cope with as they had predicted. Take Rebecca, for example, who was extremely worried about the impact that recovering from her eating disorder would have on her life. She made it clear, at the first meeting with her therapist, that she was very pessimistic about changing her eating habits, and very unsure whether or not change would be worth it. She told us that stopping bingeing and vomiting would mean that she would have

---

Box 1.1 Rebecca's experience

Rebecca's verdict: Was it worth it?

At first I thought I would never be able to stop bingeing, but my confidence grew with each success. It was hard work, particularly at the beginning, and I had some set backs along the way. At times I needed to remind myself of the benefits of keeping on with it. But I wouldn't go back to my old life now for anything. Instead of spending most evenings bingeing at home by myself, I've got a busy social life. I've found new friends at work. I've made a positive choice to stay with my partner (since stopping treatment we've got engaged). I'm no longer depressed. I've got my old sparkle back. I can cook for friends and I can go out to eat. We're planning our first holiday for three years (I've saved lots of money since I stopped bingeing).

Rebecca's views on the programme

I stopped bingeing and vomiting quite quickly; then the programme helped me give up dieting. But it didn't just help me with my eating or with the worries I had about how much I weighed. It also helped me deal with old problems in new ways. Most of all, it's been a way of changing how I see myself. After years of misery, it's transformed my life, and my view of myself, in a way I never believed possible. My only regret is that I didn't do it years ago.

to face lots of things that she was deeply unhappy about; problems that she felt would be too distressing and difficult for her to deal with.

Moreover, in the past few years Rebecca had read a great many self-help books, none of which had helped her, and she was suspicious of yet another programme. However, after completing the exercises in Chapters 5 and 6, which increased her commitment to change, she amazed herself by making excellent progress. She stopped bingeing and found new ways to deal with the problems (old and new) that emerged. Look at Box 1.1 for her verdict on whether it was worth all the effort and hard work, and for her views on the programme.

We hope Rebecca's story is reassuring if you are pessimistic about change, undecided and uncertain whether it will be worth the effort, or if you are worried about how you will cope if your eating habits improve. We hope that you will read on, and that you will find what you are looking for in this book.

Chapter summary

At the beginning of this chapter we stated that the aim of our book is to help you overcome bulimia nervosa. The following points were made about the programme in this chapter. Each is important.

- It is based on a psychological theory – cognitive theory – and a psychological treatment approach – cognitive therapy.

- It draws on recent developments by scientists and clinicians in both the theory and therapy of eating disorders.

- As you work through it, you will discover what maintains your eating disorder and why it has developed; you will learn how to use cognitive therapy strategies to overcome it.

- The programme has already helped many people. Many people can overcome their problems using self-help alone.

- You will need to commit yourself wholeheartedly to all the suggestions and exercises that are relevant to your problem and work through from start to finish.

- Eating disorders are more common in young women, but the programme is also likely to help you if you are older or male.

- At first most people feel pessimistic about recovery and worried that change might make things worse, but it is possible to change and be glad you've changed.

CHAPTER 2

Introduction to Bulimia Nervosa

In this chapter we introduce you to bulimia nervosa. The chapter will cover the key features of the disorder, the relationship between bulimia nervosa and other disorders, as well as related symptoms and problems. It will also cover the extent or prevalence of the disorder, and the significance of isolated episodes of bingeing and vomiting. First, however, we will tell you about Catherine.

Catherine

Catherine is 20 years old. She has bulimia nervosa. Catherine has been concerned about her weight and shape for several years. As a teenager she felt plump and was frequently on a diet, even though she was within the normal weight range for her age and height. As she became older, these concerns became more serious. She severely restricted her food intake and started punishing exercise regimes. At one stage she became significantly underweight. Medical help led to weight gain, which was quickly followed by more dieting and, for the first time, she started binge eating. Distressed by the increase in her weight and by increasingly frequent binge eating she began vomiting in a desperate attempt to lose weight.

Over the last six months Catherine has skipped breakfast and lunch, eaten a normal evening meal with her family, but gone on to binge eat in the late evening, usually two or three times a week. She binges in response to feeling upset and worried. In a recent, typical binge she ate four slices of toast with butter and jam, six packets of crisps, three large chocolate bars, half a box of cereal and a large bowl of ice cream. She had been feeling rejected by a friend. Catherine drinks large quantities of water to help her induce vomiting after bingeing. More recently she has started to take 30 to 40 laxatives, as well as vomiting. She has a strenuous exercise regime, including 500 daily sit-ups and an aerobic workout. Food is divided rigidly into good and bad categories; food in the bad category (such as biscuits, chocolate and cheese) is not allowed. She has become increasingly self-conscious. She refuses to weigh herself, has given up swimming (she used to swim in her school team) and if she goes shopping will not try on clothes in communal changing rooms. She dislikes her body. She is preoccupied with her shape and reports that a little voice in her head constantly says, 'You're fat and ugly, I can't stand the way you look.' Catherine worries that her friends will think less of her if she does not lose weight (when out with friends she avoids eating and sucks her tummy in to the point of pain in order to appear thinner). She also feels very bad about herself if she thinks she has gained weight.

The key features of bulimia nervosa

Since first being identified as a distinct problem in the early 1980s, bulimia nervosa has attracted a variety of different definitions. These have become increasingly refined as research and our patients tell us more about the disorder. The five key features of the definition that is now commonly used in research studies can be seen in Box 2.1. All five features are required for a diagnosis of bulimia nervosa.

Box 2.1 The five key features of bulimia nervosa

- Binge eating – eating more food in a single episode of eating than most people would normally eat in similar circumstances; a sense of loss of control over eating

- Behaviour designed to prevent weight gain, e.g. self-induced vomiting, taking large quantities of laxatives or diuretics, extreme dieting, fasting, excessive exercising (these are often called 'compensatory' behaviours).

- Binge eating (and compensatory behaviours) both occur at least twice a week, and have been going on for at least three months.

- Weight and shape play a large part in how the person evaluates herself. They are often the most or almost the most important things that make the person feel good or bad about herself.

- The person is not also very underweight.

Bulimia nervosa and related disorders

Several disorders are related to bulimia nervosa, including both eating disorders and other disorders, such as depression and borderline personality disorder. A list of these disorders can be seen in Box 2.2.

Box 2.2 Disorders related to bulimia nervosa

- Anorexia nervosa.

- Binge-eating disorder.

- Depression.

- Multi-impulsive disorder.

- Borderline personality disorder.

Anorexia nervosa

The disorder most closely associated with bulimia nervosa is anorexia nervosa, an eating disorder in which sufferers reach an extremely low weight, feel too fat despite their low weight, and are very frightened of even small amounts of weight gain. Two kinds of anorexia nervosa are usually identified, a restricting type and a bulimic type. Restrictors maintain their low weight primarily by dieting, while bulimics also have episodes of bingeing followed by compensatory behaviour. The symptoms of bulimic anorexia are very similar to those of bulimia nervosa, except that bulimic anorexics are significantly underweight. Lots of people move at different times between bulimia nervosa and one or both types of anorexia nervosa. The commonest pattern is for a person to have an initial diagnosis of anorexia nervosa, which then turns into bulimia nervosa. Some people move intermittently and repeatedly between the two disorders, particularly if their eating problem remains untreated over a period of several years. As in bulimia nervosa, weight and shape play a large part in how the person with anorexia nervosa views herself, and low self-esteem is common.

Binge-eating disorder

Binge-eating disorder has recently been formally identified as a distinct eating disorder, although it is clear that it has existed for many years. Like people with bulimia nervosa, sufferers have repeated binges in which they eat unusually large amounts of food and feel a sense of loss of control while eating. However, they don't attempt to compensate for overeating, as happens in bulimia nervosa. Sufferers are also more likely to be overweight than those with bulimia nervosa. As in bulimia nervosa, there is great distress about the binge-eating; this may include concern about weight and shape.

Depression

Depression is common in people with bulimia nervosa. While some people do seem to have a clinical depression that is relatively independent of their eating disorder, many find that their depression is closely linked to their bulimia nervosa. Typically, the depression began together with or shortly after concern about weight and shape developed and it fluctuates depending on how much the eating disorder is causing distress. When bingeing and vomiting are more severe, depression increases. When they are relatively better, mood improves. Nearly always in such cases, the depression lifts once the eating problem is resolved and does not usually need any separate treatment.

Multi-impulsive disorder

A small number of people with bulimia nervosa also have problems with alcohol or drug abuse. Others have problems with self-harm (for example, cutting or burning their skin) or spend money beyond their means. In this group, alcohol, drugs, self-harm or excessive spending, as well as bingeing, are used to deal with stress or tension, and with self-hate, self-loathing and self- disgust. It has been suggested that these people have particularly poor impulse control and this pattern of symptoms has been called 'multi-impulsive' disorder.

Borderline personality disorder

Some people with bulimia nervosa (again, probably only a small number) have some symptoms that are typical of borderline personality disorder. Typically, these symptoms describe deeply ingrained, life long patterns of behaving (dating back to early life) and are considered to be part of a person's character or 'personality' rather than a specific illness. When they are chronic, the term borderline personality disorder (the name is simply a historical legacy) is used to describe the symptoms that can be seen in Box 2.3.

While one or more of the symptoms in Box 2.3 may be present in bulimia nervosa, it is usually unclear whether they existed before the eating disorder (i.e. are truly long standing and part of a person's character), or whether they are simply the result of having bulimia nervosa. Research suggests that, in most cases, they seem to be a consequence of bulimia nervosa and, once the eating disorder has resolved, they simply disappear.

Box 2.3 Key borderline personality disorder symptoms

- Unstable and intense relationships, e.g. alternating between extreme idealisation and extreme devaluation of other people, fears of abandonment.

- Identity disturbance, e.g. unstable sense of self, poor self-image.

- Impulsive, self-damaging behaviour, e.g. spending beyond means, reckless driving, binge eating, risky sexual behaviour.

- Repeated suicidal threats or attempts; self-mutilating behaviour.

- Intense and marked mood shifts, e.g. in anxiety, depression, or difficulty in controlling anger.

- Long-standing feelings of emptiness.

Associated symptoms and problems

In addition to the key defining features, bulimia nervosa is associated with several other symptoms and problems. The main ones are discussed below.

Dieting

Strict dieting is typical of bulimia nervosa. Three types of dieting are often identified. These are avoiding eating, restricting the overall amount of food eaten and avoiding certain 'bad' (usually high calorie) foods.

Demoralisation

Dieting is often closely linked to demoralisation. People who binge usually try to stick to extremely strict diets, in between episodes of bingeing. However, as all dieters know, it is difficult to be successful with very strict diets and repeated failures are common. Failure is demoralising and diet breaking tends to enhance both low self-esteem and the feeling of being out of control around food. Demoralisation can also occur with repeated attempts and failures to recover.

Obsessive thoughts

People with bulimia nervosa are invariably preoccupied with thoughts of food and eating, weight and shape. These thoughts are often distracting and distressing. They may mean that sufferers can't concentrate on the many other things that they would like to be doing or thinking about. These thoughts may arise from concern about weight and shape or from dieting. Dieting, in particular, means being constantly alert to food and eating; it requires great attention and concentration. Preoccupation with weight and shape and with food and eating often leads to considerable frustration at the inability to think about anything else.

Body shape

Body shape is extremely important to people with bulimia nervosa. Although the research on body size is inconclusive – it is not clear whether, as is sometimes suggested, people with eating disorders overestimate their true size – most feel overweight and think that they are too fat. As suggested above, most also focus on and think about their body size and shape a great deal. Often, a particular part of the body, such as the stomach, hips or thighs, causes most concern.

Behaviours

People with bulimia nervosa frequently engage in a variety of checking behaviours connected with their weight and shape. For example, they may weigh themselves frequently in order to see whether or not they have gained weight, or they may check or measure body parts to see if they are getting fatter or thinner. The opposite, putting a lot of effort into trying not to do these things, often occurs as well. For example, a person may refuse to put herself into situations where she might be confronted with her own weight and shape or, in comparison, with that of others. Thus she might refuse to weigh herself, avoid changing in communal changing rooms, avoid swimming, and avoid wearing tight clothes. Sometimes people fluctuate between checking and avoidance at different times, depending on whether or not they have recently gained or lost weight.

Self-esteem

Although it is not usually considered a key or defining feature, our research and clinical experience indicate that people with bulimia nervosa nearly always have a very low opinion of themselves and poor self-worth. They frequently feel a failure, worthless, no good, bad and unlovable and they may feel all alone. Poor self-esteem (which reflects what, in our research and clinical practice, we call negative self-beliefs) is a crucial aspect of eating disorders. Our experience suggests that it often predates bulimia nervosa and that it is vital to help people with bulimia nervosa feel better about themselves in order for recovery to be complete.

Early experience

People with bulimia nervosa have often been deeply affected by some of their early childhood or early teenage experiences. These experiences may be very traumatic and may include sexual, physical and emotional abuse. Other experiences may appear objectively less serious or traumatic but have, nonetheless, left lasting scars.

For example, some people with bulimia nervosa report being teased or bullied at school, or feeling different from peers because of particular family circumstances. Such experiences often coincide with the person's first memory of feeling bad about themselves, and those people often make a link between how they were treated as a child and the development of their low self-esteem. Many people also report negative experiences related to food and eating, weight and shape, usually at a rather later date, that coincide with the beginning of their difficulties with eating or increased concern about weight and shape. This may include feeling different from peers because of maturational changes in body shape.

Children

The children of those with bulimia nervosa may be affected. There may be attempts to restrict their food intake as well, or simply a lack of food available for them because of attempts to avoid bingeing by keeping very little food in the house. Daughters, in particular, may suffer as they get older and may feel under pressure to join in a mother's dieting. Mothers with bulimia nervosa can also overfeed as well as underfeed their children. This is usually because they find it difficult to judge what normal eating looks like.

The law

Occasionally, people with bulimia nervosa shoplift and, as a result, may end up involved with the law. Often, it is food that is stolen but other items, particularly clothes, may be taken as well.

Finance

Bingeing can be an expensive burden and may lead to financial difficulties. At worst, considerable debts can be accumulated so that there is not enough money for essentials, such as rent or mortgage payments, gas and electricity bills. At best, it often means that treats, such as a special holiday, regular nights out or special presents for family or friends cannot be afforded. Often this happens because people with bulimia nervosa run up debts on credit and store cards; buying clothes, to 'cheer themselves up' or to make themselves feel better about their weight and shape.

Work and studying

Performance at work or college may be affected. Some may be so disabled by bulimia nervosa that they are unable to work or undertake further education. Low self-esteem, as well as the time and effort taken up by bingeing, may also be a barrier to work or study. Some of those who do work or are studying may be underachieving because of their eating disorder. Others may throw all their energy into this aspect of their lives and be high achievers, often at the expense of the rest of their lives, driven by a desire for perfection or outstanding achievement.

Accommodation

Many young people live in shared accommodation; sometimes with friends, sometimes with people they do not know so well. Bingeing can create severe tension in such circumstances. Stealing food from housemates or friends for a binge is not uncommon and may lead to strain on relationships. In some circumstances, it may lead to a request from housemates or friends for the person to move out.

Social life and relationships

Bulimia nervosa is a very lonely disorder; the secrecy, guilt and shame felt about it frequently lead to isolation from other people and overall quality of social life and intimate relationships may be poor. There is often a tendency to avoid social contact and social occasions, particularly when food is involved. This can be hurtful to friends and family. With time, relationships may fail or not be sustained, either because the eating disorder takes up so much time and attention or because of the need to hide essential details of the problem from other people.

In families, or with partners, bulimia nervosa can lead to tension and arguments about the disappearance of food, the financial cost of bingeing and the sufferer's apparent inability to take part in normal activities. The family or partner may put pressure on the sufferer to change and become angry and resentful when she appears unable to do so. In the end, some families and partners just adapt to the disorder, especially if it has been going on for some time. Although this places less pressure on the sufferer, it may engender a hopeless attitude and convey the message that they have given up hope of a return to normal life.

The prevalence of bulimia nervosa

Research suggests that bulimia nervosa occurs mostly in young women. It is more common in industrialised western countries and in those from professional, upper- and middle-class families. At present, it seems to be less common among women from ethnic minorities. Studies of the general population, not restricted to patients (who may, for a variety of reasons, be a select group) suggest that at any one time between 1 per cent and 2 per cent of adolescent and young women have bulimia nervosa. This figure is almost certainly greater in certain 'at risk' groups, for example, dancers, gymnasts and fashion models. Among those who treat women with bulimia nervosa, the general impression is that it is becoming much more common and much more widespread. More women from ethnic minorities and from working and lower middle class families are now coming forward for treatment. There also appears to be a small but growing number of young men and older women with the disorder.

Bulimia nervosa and normal dieting

At any one time a large and apparently increasing number of adolescent and young women are dieting in order to lose weight. Dieting is a key feature of bulimia nervosa but, clearly, the vast majority of women who diet do not develop an eating disorder. However, research does indicate that it is a risk factor. If you have been on and off diets for much of your life you are more likely to develop bulimia nervosa than someone who has never or seldom dieted. Nevertheless, no one is very certain why or how constant dieting turns into bulimia nervosa. We have some tentative ideas based on our recent research. In brief, this suggests that dieting becomes bulimia nervosa, or makes it more likely, when two conditions are met:

1. The person is highly concerned about her weight, shape and eating, to the extent that it is one of the most important things that makes her feel good or bad about herself.

2. These concerns exist together with or develop in the context of extremely low self-esteem.

It is the existence of both that can trigger or turn dieting into bulimia nervosa.

Isolated episodes of bingeing and vomiting

Single or infrequent episodes of bingeing followed by compensatory behaviour will mean that you do not meet the generally accepted criteria for a diagnosis of bulimia nervosa. For some people infrequent binges may not be problematic. However, for other people isolated or infrequent episodes of bingeing are accompanied by much distress. In such cases the person is nearly always a chronic dieter and usually extremely concerned about her eating, weight and shape. We know relatively little about this group of people. Our impression is that some, at least, may be protected from developing a full-blown eating disorder by relatively good general self-esteem. If you binge and vomit only infrequently but you are distressed by your behaviour, if it interferes with your life and you want to stop doing it, you may still find the cognitive therapy strategies and skills presented in this book helpful.

Plan of the book

This chapter has introduced you to bulimia nervosa. Among other things, the next chapter will introduce cognitive theory, the theory behind our programme. We will then help you to determine if you have bulimia nervosa and how the programme can help you. After that, the programme will cover encouraging yourself to change. More detail will then be provided on the model on which the programme is based. We will move on to help you draw up the vicious circle of thoughts, feelings and behaviours that maintains your own episodes of binge eating.

Next, you will learn how you can begin to get control of your eating by identifying and challenging key problematic thoughts. Behaviours (such as strict dieting and frequent weighing) that maintain negative thoughts about weight and shape will also be identified, and your fears about giving them up will be tested out in practice.

The chapters that follow will help you to examine your beliefs about eating, weight and shape and about yourself. They will also help you to break the link between dieting and self-worth, as well as help you to improve your general sense of overall self-worth. At the very end of the programme, how to prevent relapse and preparing for the future will be addressed. Each chapter builds on the one before, with the aim of taking one step at a time.

Chapter summary

This chapter has introduced you to bulimia nervosa. The important points covered include the following:

- Bulimia nervosa is binge eating followed by compensatory behaviour; it should have been occurring twice a week for at least three months; weight and shape play a large part in self-evaluation; the person is not very underweight.

- Bulimia nervosa is related to several other disorders, including anorexia nervosa, binge-eating disorder and depression. Very occasionally it might be related to multi-impulsive disorder and borderline personality disorder.

- Many symptoms and problems are associated with the disorder; low self-esteem is particularly important.

- Bulimia nervosa occurs mostly in young women, but is becoming more widespread.

- It is different from normal dieting; only a minority of dieters develop eating disorders.

- Those who binge and vomit infrequently may not be particularly distressed by their behaviour unless, like those with bulimia nervosa, they also have low self-esteem.

The chapter has also outlined the plan of the book. It has emphasised the programme's step-by-step approach.

CHAPTER 3

Do I have
Bulimia Nervosa?

If you are having problems with your eating then you are probably asking yourself by now, how do I tell if I have bulimia nervosa? This chapter will help you to find out. By the end you will be able to tell if you have bulimia nervosa, a related disorder or, if not full-blown bulimia nervosa, whether you may be at risk of developing it. You will also be able to tell whether you have any other significant problems.

Questionnaire: Do I have bulimia nervosa?

Completing Questionnaire 3.1 will tell you whether it is likely that you have bulimia nervosa. It is in the form of a 'decision tree'. Answer each question as 'yes' or 'no' and follow the 'yes' and 'no' arrows until you reach a 'no' box (signalling that you are unlikely to have bulimia nervosa), or the 'yes' box at the bottom of the tree (signalling that you may well have bulimia nervosa). Along the way the tree will also tell you whether you might have binge-eating disorder or the bulimic form of anorexia nervosa. You will probably need to know your body mass index (BMI) in order to work out which type of eating disorder you have. Use the table and formula in Appendix 1 (p.203) to work out your BMI before you start. Do try to answer the questions as accurately and as honestly as possible. Remember that hiding the extent or nature of your eating problem from yourself will not help you to help yourself get better.

The significance of different scores

Bulimia nervosa

If you reached the bottom of the decision tree then you almost certainly have bulimia nervosa. This means that the programme is very likely to help you.

AT RISK OF BULIMIA NERVOSA

If you reached the 'at risk' box then, although you do not strictly speaking have bulimia nervosa you have many of the symptoms and may well be at a greater risk of developing it. This is particularly likely if you also have low self-esteem. The programme is very likely to help you too.

Questionnaire 3.1 Do I have bulimia nervosa?

Do I binge eat?

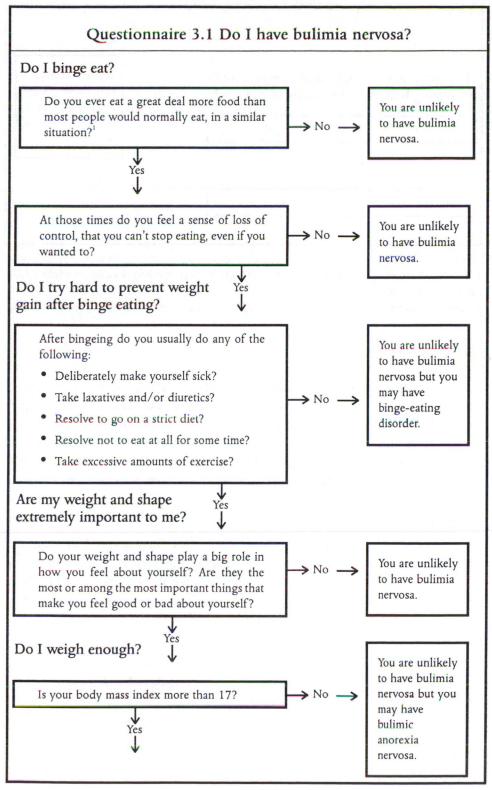

Do you ever eat a great deal more food than most people would normally eat, in a similar situation?[1] → No → You are unlikely to have bulimia nervosa.

↓ Yes

At those times do you feel a sense of loss of control, that you can't stop eating, even if you wanted to? → No → You are unlikely to have bulimia nervosa.

Do I try hard to prevent weight gain after binge eating?

↓ Yes

After bingeing do you usually do any of the following:

- Deliberately make yourself sick?
- Take laxatives and/or diuretics?
- Resolve to go on a strict diet?
- Resolve not to eat at all for some time?
- Take excessive amounts of exercise?

→ No → You are unlikely to have bulimia nervosa but you may have binge-eating disorder.

Are my weight and shape extremely important to me?

↓ Yes

Do your weight and shape play a big role in how you feel about yourself? Are they the most or among the most important things that make you feel good or bad about yourself? → No → You are unlikely to have bulimia nervosa.

Do I weigh enough?

↓ Yes

Is your body mass index more than 17? → No → You are unlikely to have bulimia nervosa but you may have bulimic anorexia nervosa.

↓ Yes

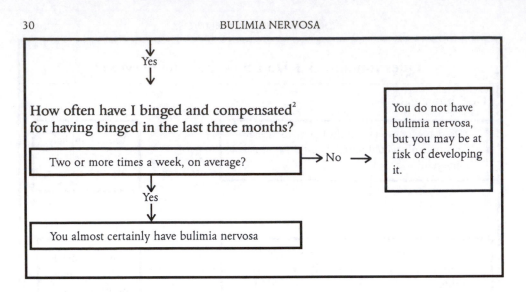

1. In addition to this criterion, a binge is usually defined as an episode of eating in which 1,000 calories or more are consumed.
2. Compensated means engaged in behaviours to prevent weight gain, such as vomiting, taking laxatives, excessive exercise etc.

FREQUENCY OF BINGEING

In determining whether you have bulimia nervosa or are simply 'at risk', remember to take into account any unusual circumstances that may have affected your eating in the last three months. For example, you may have been on holiday with other people for part of that time, or living somewhere where it was very difficult to binge eat. If you know that you would have binged and compensated for bingeing if you had been in your usual surroundings, then it is very likely that you have bulimia nervosa.

Bulimic anorexia nervosa

If you reached this box then you may have the bulimic form of anorexia nervosa. It is very similar to bulimia nervosa but, as well as bingeing, your weight is unhealthily low. You may well find the programme useful but we also urge you to seek advice from your general practitioner (GP) or from your family doctor or physician before you start; being at a very low weight can be very dangerous.

Binge-eating disorder

If you reached this box then you may have binge-eating disorder. A great deal of the programme may well be helpful to you.

Other eating problems

It is possible that after completing the questionnaire you discover that, although your eating difficulties and concerns are extremely distressing and disabling, you do not seem to fit into any of the eating disorder categories described so far. One possibility is that you have the restricting form of anorexia nervosa. If this seems likely then you should seek professional help. Another possibility is that you have symptoms typical of several different types of eating disorder, or your symptoms fluctuate and change frequently, so that you shift between different disorders. Researchers and clinicians have noted that this can happen, although we do not know how common it is. If this describes you then you may have a non-specific eating disorder. You can check your symptoms against those in Box 3.1.

Box 3.1 The key symptoms of non-specific eating disorders

- All the symptoms of anorexia nervosa except that menstruation has not stopped or, despite marked weight loss, weight remains in the normal range

- All the symptoms of bulimia nervosa except that binge-eating and compensatory behaviour do not occur often enough or have not been going on for long enough

- Compensates for eating small amounts of food, e.g. vomits after eating two biscuits

- Frequently chews and spits out, and does not swallow, large amounts of food

---

If part of your non-specific eating problem is binge-eating, then the programme may still be helpful to you. What if you are having difficulties with your eating, but do not seem to fit into any of the categories mentioned so far? Well, you have almost certainly ruled out several possible reasons for your problems. However, so that your problems can be identified and treated appropriately, we strongly urge you to seek professional advice. At the present time we recommend that you see your general practitioner (GP), family doctor or physician.

Medication

If you have consulted a medical doctor about your eating problems then you may have been offered Prozac; indeed you may well be taking it regularly. Prozac is an effective treatment for many people with bulimia nervosa. Nevertheless, it does not help everyone and for some people it is only of limited help. If you are taking Prozac but are still having difficulties with your eating, then there is no reason why you should not also follow our programme. However, do remember that if you are taking Prozac regularly, you should not stop taking it or change the doseage without consulting the doctor who prescribed it.

Suitability of the book for the reader

By now you should have a good idea whether or not you have bulimia nervosa, as it is usually defined. If completing Questionnaire 3.1 has confirmed that you do indeed have bulimia nervosa, then the self-help programme is likely to be extremely suitable for you. It may also be of help if the only reason you do not fit into the bulimia nervosa category is because your problem, however distressing, does not occur frequently enough; that is, if you are 'at risk'. It may also be useful if you have bulimic anorexia nervosa or binge-eating disorder, or a non-specific eating disorder that involves binge eating.

Additional problems

By now you will have discovered whether the self-help programme is likely to be suitable for you. However, before going ahead it is also important to ask yourself whether you have any other significant difficulties, apart from your eating problem. Sometimes the presence of other problems may mean that you could find it difficult to benefit fully from the programme without some additional help. Completing Questionnaire 3.2 will help you to work out whether you have any other significant difficulties. Read through each question and circle the 'yes' box on the right if your answer is yes. We will then discuss whether you should seek help in addition to following the programme.

When additional help is needed

If you have answered yes to one or more of the questions on Questionnaire 3.2 then it may be advisable for you to seek additional (professional) help, as well as following the self-help programme. It is particularly important that you do so if you often feel that life isn't worth living or if you are regularly harming yourself. You may also find it difficult to overcome your eating problem by yourself if you are feeling very depressed, or in an abusive relationship. Finally, professional support and advice may help you to minimise the impact of any legal, financial and school or work difficulties that are related to your eating problem.

Questionnaire 3.2 Do I have additional significant problems?

Am I extremely depressed?

Do you feel very down just about all of the time?	Yes
Have you lost all interest in the things you usually enjoy?	Yes

Am I feeling completely hopeless?

Do you feel life isn't worth living?	Yes
Have you made plans to harm yourself?	Yes

Am I harming myself at the moment?

Do you often drink too much alcohol?	Yes
Do you regularly take illegal drugs?	Yes
Do you regularly cut or burn your skin?	Yes
Do you often take overdoses of prescribed or over the counter medication?	Yes

Am I in a violent or abusive relationship?

Does your partner abuse you, physically, sexually or emotionally?	Yes
Does someone else in your life abuse you?	Yes

Am I involved with the law?

Has your eating problem contributed to on-going legal action against you?	Yes

Am I in severe financial difficulties?

Is the expense of your eating problem causing you severe problems with money, for example, with mortgage lenders, credit card companies?	Yes

Am I in danger of failing exams or losing my job?

Are you failing badly at school or college because of your eating problem?	Yes
Is your job performance severely affected by your eating problem (for example, you've received warning letters or been threatened with dismissal)?	Yes

Plans to harm yourself

If you have answered yes to the question 'Have you made plans to harm yourself?', then you are probably feeling extremely hopeless as well as very depressed. In such circumstances it is absolutely vital that you seek help from your GP, family doctor or physician as soon as possible.

Sexual, physical and emotional abuse

If you suffered abuse as a child you may also want to consider whether it would be useful to seek professional advice. You may find it particularly useful when you get to later sections of the book. It may be hard, for example, for you to revisit your early experiences in the ways we suggest on your own. This is especially true in Chapters 17 and 18, which deal with core beliefs.

How to find additional help

The first port of call for professional help in the UK within the NHS is usually your GP (in the USA you should consult your family doctor or physician). Your GP can refer you either to a Community Mental Health Team (CMHT), usually consisting of a range of mental health professionals, such as clinical psychologists, psychiatrists, Community Psychiatric Nurses (CPNs), social workers, or, if it is available locally, to a specialist eating disorder service. They may also be able to refer you to a local clinical psychology department providing services outside a CMHT. The advantage of this is that many clinical psychologists are trained in cognitive therapy. Some GP practices also have counsellors attached to the local surgery who have experience of treating eating disorders and of cognitive therapy. If you are a student your university or college may have a counselling service that you can use. You may also find the support of national self-help organisations useful. Some of these organisations produce newsletters and run local groups. Contact details for national groups in Europe, Australia, New Zealand and the USA can be found in Appendix 5.

Self-help and additional help

If you are referred for further help, particularly to a cognitive therapist, then portions of the programme may still be helpful, as an adjunct to either individual or group therapy.

Chapter summary

This chapter has helped you find out whether you have bulimia nervosa and whether, if you do, you have any other significant problems. The following important points were made:

- If you have bulimia nervosa (or if you are 'at risk') then the book may well help you.

- It may also be helpful if you have bulimic anorexia nervosa, binge-eating disorder or a non-specific eating disorder that involves binge eating.

- If you think you may have bulimic (or restricting) anorexia nervosa, then you should seek professional advice.

- If you have bulimia nervosa together with other significant difficulties, then you should also seek professional help. This is vital if you have made plans to harm yourself.

- You may still be able to use the manual, or portions of it, if additional help is needed; this is particularly likely if you find a therapist trained in cognitive therapy.

CHAPTER 4

Theories of Bulimia Nervosa

Several different theories or explanations of bulimia nervosa exist, in addition to the cognitive explanation on which our programme is based. In this chapter we introduce you briefly to the main theories including, towards the end of the chapter, cognitive theory.

A form of depression

Some eating disorder experts have argued that eating disorders are forms of depression. However, descriptions of clinical features, the family history of people with eating disorders and depression, response to anti-depressant drugs and neuro-biological findings do not, on the whole, fit with this theory and it is now largely discredited.

A personality disorder

It has been argued that some symptoms of bulimia nervosa, for example, frequent mood changes and poor impulse control, suggest an underlying personality disorder, rather than a specific eating disorder illness. This implies that the problem, at its roots, is an integral part of a person's character and may, therefore, be difficult to change. There is little evidence for this view; many of the symptoms that suggest a personality disorder are now thought to be a consequence of bulimia nervosa and, like depression, often disappear once the eating disorder is resolved.

Socio-cultural models

The more women diet, the more likely they are to develop an eating disorder. Socio-cultural models attribute the rise of dieting to society's emphasis on appearance, weight and shape, especially to the focus on thinness. Because social pressure about weight is greater for women than for men, this explains why women generally develop bulimia nervosa. However, sociocultural models do not explain why only a minority of dieters develop an eating disorder. Research suggests that dieting is a necessary precursor to the illness but is not sufficient in itself to cause it. Other factors besides dieting also seem to place a person at risk of developing an eating disorder, including a higher body weight, perceived social problems, introversion and a family psychiatric history.

Developmental theories

Developmental theories explain why eating disorders often originate in adolescence. They focus mainly on adolescent development largely within the theoretical framework originally developed by Sigmund Freud. They emphasise adolescent turmoil, the development of self-concept and body-concept and the formation of identity, all of which are taking place at this time.

Developmental theorists argue that social and cultural pressure on women to be thin is greatest in teenage years and in the early twenties when women are developing physically, socially and emotionally.

There is also some evidence that the stress of adolescence creates greater inner turmoil in girls than boys, leaving them more miserable, anxious, insecure, self-conscious and with lower self-esteem than boys. These factors, it is argued, make girls more vulnerable than boys to the effects of pressure to be thin, and more likely to develop a body concept and self-concept, highly influenced by weight and shape. Indeed, it is often at this stage that controlling weight and shape becomes a means for girls to feel better about themselves.

Developmental theories also suggest that, in general, forming an identity is often more difficult for girls than boys. They point out that girls are, in modern societies, vulnerable to conflicting and rapidly changing views of women, particularly in areas of food, feeding, body consciousness, developing sexuality and sex roles. This also helps to explain why girls are more likely than boys to end up searching for and defining their identity in terms of weight and shape.

Family systems

The idea of a disturbed family system as a cause or maintaining factor in eating disorders has been around for a long time. Although experience suggests that there are some differences between the families of those with bulimia nervosa and those without in how conflict is resolved, this could well be a correlate or consequence of the eating disorder rather than a cause.

Biological hypotheses

Three main biological hypotheses have been proposed. The first suggests a deficiency in serotonin, a chemical responsible for facilitating communication between cells in the brain. The second suggests an abnormality in electrical impulses in the brain; also responsible for communication in the brain. Both theories now seem unlikely. The third suggests that people with bulimia nervosa have an abnormal response to signs of fullness in the stomach. It now seems likely that this is a consequence rather than a cause of bulimia nervosa.

Genetic links

Research suggests that eating disorders (and also depression) are more common in the relatives of those with bulimia nervosa than might be expected. This could reflect the fact that close relatives often grow up in similar circumstances, rather than indicating a straightforward genetic link. However, although little research has yet been carried out, some work with identical and non-identical twins provides some tentative evidence for such a link in anorexia nervosa.

Cognitive theory

Cognitive theory looks in detail at the thoughts (cognitions), feelings and behaviours that keep bulimia nervosa going on a moment-by-moment basis. Thoughts, feelings and behaviour are closely linked, often in the form of vicious circles. Cognitive theory places particular emphasis on thoughts and, in cognitive therapy for bulimia nervosa, the key to overcoming distressing behaviour and feelings lies in identifying and finding ways to challenge and change negative thoughts. This will interrupt the vicious circle(s) of thoughts, feelings and behaviour: with practice, it will also change feelings and ways of behaving. As you will discover there are several ways of changing feelings and behaviour (more on this later). As we also hope you will discover, identifying and challenging thoughts is a powerful way to interrupt and, eventually, to prevent the downward spiral of distress that can occur in bulimia nervosa.

Cognitive theory and other theories

Cognitive theory is not necessarily incompatible with other theories. In many cases different theories are simply dealing with different aspects or different levels of the problem. For example, the psychological features (thoughts, feelings and behaviours) of cognitive theory could be expressed in terms of biological or genetic features; or they could be seen to be a result of difficulty in resolving developmental issues, together with societal emphasis on women to be thin.

One of the advantages of cognitive theory is that it captures the person's own experience of their problem; it uses their language to understand personal thoughts, feelings and behaviour. Moreover, once the problem is understood in these terms and the key thoughts have been identified, then the theory leads directly into strategies for change. Importantly, unlike most other theories of eating disorders, the cognitive model of bulimia nervosa and the treatment based on it, cognitive therapy, has been widely investigated and is supported by a considerable amount of research.

Chapter summary

This chapter has introduced you to some of the theories that explain bulimia nervosa. This has included an introduction to cognitive theory, which forms the basis for our book. Important points covered include the following:

- There are many theories of bulimia nervosa
- Cognitive theory focuses particularly on thoughts
- In cognitive theory thoughts give rise to feelings and behaviours
- Thoughts, feelings and behaviours are linked in bulimia nervosa in the form of vicious circles; these maintain the disorder on a moment by moment basis
- Cognitive therapy seeks to change distressing feelings and problem behaviours by identifying and challenging the thoughts associated with them
- Cognitive theory is not necessarily incompatible with other theories.

PART 2

The Programme

A note before you start

Using the programme

People progress at different rates through the programme, and you may need to spend longer on some sections of it than on others. Quite often it will be helpful to read sections more than once and to practice exercises several times before you move on. Depending on your particular problems, some sections may also be more help to you than others. Bulimia nervosa is a complex problem and there is a lot to take in and understand. *Take it slowly* and try not to be hard on yourself if you don't understand everything immediately or if you have setbacks along the way.

A therapy file

There are lots of exercises and worksheets to complete in our programme. There are also summaries to be made and diaries to keep. You may find it useful to photocopy the blank worksheets (copies are in Appendix 2) so that, where necessary, you can make several copies of each to fill in as and when you need. Find yourself a file in which you can keep all these together, so that you don't lose any of your hard work. The file will be particularly helpful for reminding you about key points and in reviewing useful exercises. It will also be helpful if you have any setbacks. It can serve as a reminder of how you overcame the problem before. Remember that it is normal to have setbacks and normal to need to review and repeat earlier exercises to get back on track again.

A suggested timescale

You may be wondering how quickly you should work through the programme. As a rough guide we suggest that you work through the early chapters (Chapters 6 to 14) at the rate of *one chapter each week*. Later (Chapters 15 to 19) you should aim to work through *one chapter every two weeks*. This will give you time to assimilate the material and complete the later exercises over a more extended period.

Remember, this is only a rough guide. The most important thing is to read all the material and complete all the relevant exercises before you move on to a new chapter.

CHAPTER 5

Encouraging Change

Change is rarely easy when you have bulimia nervosa. Sometimes, even when you are very distressed about your eating, it may seem much easier to stay as you are. In this chapter we will ask you to complete some exercises and read some information designed to encourage you to change. The exercises include specifying your problems and goals. The information includes a discussion of common fears that might be preventing you from changing, and details of the physical consequences and dangers of bulimia nervosa.

A warning

You may think that you are very motivated to change and can skip over this chapter. However, we would advise you to read it and complete all the exercises. The chapter contains information that will be essential later on and your completed exercises will come in useful if things get difficult (as they may well at some point). Our patients often find it particularly useful to refer back to the exercises in this (and the next) chapter at such times. It helps encourage and motivate them to continue.

Exercise: Encouraging change

This exercise is designed to encourage you to change. It asks you to do two things: draw up a detailed problem list and specify your goals. Use Worksheet 5.1 and follow the steps below to complete it.

Step 1: Drawing up a problem list

In the left-hand column, under 'problems', draw up a detailed list of all the problems that you have in relation to your eating disorder. Make sure that you include all the things about your eating that are making you unhappy. Problems typically occur in four areas (Box 5.1).

Worksheet 5.1 Problems and Goals	
Problems	Goals

Box 5.1 Typical problem areas

- Binge eating

- Compensatory behaviours (vomiting, excessive use of laxatives/diuretics, excessive exercise, fasting)

- Dieting

- Obsessive thoughts and concerns about food and eating, weight and shape

Even though bingeing and vomiting (or other compensatory behaviours) may be worrying you most, try to think beyond them to any problems in the other categories (especially attempts to diet and any negative thoughts and concerns about food and eating, and about your weight and shape). These are easily overlooked as a source of problems and distress. When considering dieting, remember to think about the different ways in which you diet. These may include not eating certain foods, avoiding meals, or setting a very strict calorie limit for each day. Finally, ask yourself whether you have any other problems in relation to your eating disorder.

You may find it helpful to use the four categories in Box 5.1 as headings, with an additional 'other' heading for any other problems. You may also find it helpful to look in Box 5.2 at Sarah's list of problems. Like most people with bulimia nervosa Sarah had problems that were making her unhappy in all four areas, plus some additional, 'other' problems.

Box 5.2 Sarah's problem list

Binge eating

- The urge to binge is stronger than the urge to resist – I can't stop myself.

- The more I do it, the more I want to carry on with it.

- I'm always short of money – bingeing is costing me money I need for other things – I'm getting into debt on my credit card.

- It takes up lots of time – I don't have time for the things I used to enjoy doing.

- It restricts my social life – I can't eat with friends or go to parties.

Compensatory behaviours

Vomiting

- Vomiting is affecting my teeth – the dentist said my enamel is wearing away (more about this later).

- It's messy and embarrassing.

- It's affecting my fluid balance, especially my potassium levels (more about this later).

Laxatives

- My heart races.

- I feel giddy.

- I've fainted twice.

- I get stomach pains.

Box 5.2 continued

Dieting

- Chocolate, crisps, cake and other 'bad' foods aren't allowed.

- I put off eating until the very last minute – and get very hungry, which makes it easier to binge.

- My eating pattern is chaotic.

- I can't eat in public places, e.g. restaurants, cafés.

Negative thoughts and concerns

- I'm constantly preoccupied by thoughts of how much I weigh.

- I'm convinced that if I gain weight other people won't want to know me.

- I avoid weighing myself in case my weight has gone up.

- I'm always adding up the calories in everything I eat.

- I can't stop thinking about food and how much I've eaten.

Other

- I'm anxious about the children – how they're coping with my problem.

- I'm worried that my partner doesn't understand what's going on.

- I feel anxious and depressed.

- I'm always apologising for myself.

Write down your own particular problems and, once you are satisfied that your list is complete, turn to the next step, setting goals.

Step 2: Setting goals

Turning problems into goals is an important and useful first step in overcoming your problems. Thinking only about problems does not offer a ready solution or direction for getting better. By turning your problems into goals you can give yourself something concrete to aim for. You can then consider, with the help of this book, ways of achieving your goals.

Turn to the right-hand column of your worksheet, headed 'goals'. For each problem that you have identified, generate one or more concrete goals that, when you have reached them, will tell you that you have overcome the problem. Try to make your goals as specific as possible. If they are too general you will not know when you have reached them.

Sarah decided that she wanted to be able to eat normally (as you can see in Box 5.2 one of her problems was that her eating pattern was chaotic). First, however, she had to work out what eating normally would look like. After several years of binge eating this wasn't particularly easy. To help herself, she thought about what and how much her friends ate. After some deliberation she concluded that eating normally was 'eating a normal diet and eating at regular intervals (a minimum of three times a day)'. She also concluded that 'meals should consist of a range of food and portion sizes should be similar to those of people my own age'.

Useful questions to help you to identify what your goals might be in each of the four categories (with bingeing and dieting collapsed into one category) can be seen in Box 5.3.

Use this style of questioning to help you identify goals for problems that fall into the 'other' category too. You may also find it useful to look at Jackie's problem list and the goals she generated for each problem. Her problems and goals can be seen in Box 5.4. You will see that, in addition to wanting to stop bingeing and spend more time on other things, she had two additional goals in the bingeing category: she wanted to understand what kept her bingeing going and she wanted to reduce the urge to binge. Add in any additional goals you may have in each category, just as Jackie did.

Box 5.3 Questions to identify goals

- **Bingeing and dieting:** What would you like your eating habits to be like? What would you like to be doing instead of bingeing and dieting?

- **Compensatory behaviours:** How would you like to change extreme methods of weight control? What would you like to be doing instead?

- **Obsessive thoughts and concerns about food and eating, weight and shape:** How would you like to think about food and eating, weight and shape? What would you like to be doing instead of spending so much time thinking about food and eating, and your weight and shape?

Box 5.4 Jackie's problems and goals

Problem	Goals
Bingeing • Binge eating • It takes up a lot of my spare time – I've given up my hobbies. • Don't do other things, e.g. with friends – feel I'm losing out. • My relationship with my family and friends is suffering.	• To stop bingeing and to eat normally (see below for what normal means). • To stop bingeing and spend more time on my old interests, e.g. take up badminton again, once or twice a week. • To stop bingeing and spend more time going out with my friends, e.g. go to the cinema once a week with a friend. • To rebuild contact with my family and friends, e.g. talk to my parents on the phone once a week. **Additional goals** • To understand what keeps my bingeing going. • To reduce the urge to binge.
Compensatory behaviours • Same as for bingeing.	• To stop vomiting.
Dieting • Dividing food into safe and unsafe foods, only comfortable eating fruit, salad and vegetables. • Continual dieting, e.g. planning a diet a week ahead. • Calorie counting, spending ages reading supermarket labels, buying only low calorie foods.	• To eat a normal healthy vegetarian diet that is unrestricted and similar to that of my friends (three meals a day and supper). • To stop dieting and planning diets; to plan more interesting things to do, e.g. activities with friends and family. • To stop counting calories, to stop reading calorie values when shopping, to buy food I like rather than only low calorie food.
Obsessive thoughts and concerns • Checking and counting how many calories I've eaten many, many times throughout the day. • Dislike my shape, curves and fat. • Weight loss = achievement. Weight gain = failure. • Self-conscious about my shape; try to conceal it. • Others will notice changes in my weight, like me less if I gain weight.	• To be able to use this time to read, watch television. • To feel happy and confident about myself within a normal weight range. • To discover experiences of achievement other than weight loss, e.g. in getting on well with friends, in sport, in furthering my career. • To feel less concerned about others' opinions of me; to be able to wear tighter fitting clothes, to go swimming again when on holiday. • As above.
Other problems • I'm a perfectionist.	• To learn to accept that being 'good enough' some of the time is OK, e.g. not spend long hours perfecting my reports at work.

Set realistic goals

Try to be realistic about your goals, taking into account your lifestyle and any individual circumstances. In particular, make sure that your goals are not going to make your eating disorder worse. For example, trying to reach a very low weight and cutting out 'bad' foods such as cheese or chocolate might not be helpful. A useful question to ask is: 'Would these goals be realistic if I were helping a friend overcome bulimia nervosa?' Some of the goals our patients have decided were unrealistic when they asked themselves this question can be seen in Box 5.5.

Fears about change

You are bound to have some fears about giving up your eating disorder – most people do. However, in nearly every case these fears turn out to be unfounded. We will discuss common fears below.

Weight gain

Typically, the biggest fear is that giving up bingeing and vomiting (or other extreme methods of weight control) will lead to weight gain. However, this is very unlikely to happen. People who have been helped by cognitive therapy don't usually weigh any more at the end of treatment than they did at the beginning. The reason for this is because extreme methods of weight control are not very effective. Self-induced vomiting, for example, results in the retrieval of less than half the calories eaten. This means that a large number of calories are likely to be retained in a typical binge. Other extreme methods of weight control, such as taking large quantities of laxatives and diuretics, have little or no effect on calorie absorption. Diuretics, in particular, have no effect at all. Although taken by only a minority, there is also no evidence that diet pills are helpful in bulimia nervosa. Finally, excessive exercise, while it burns off some calories, is unlikely to burn off all the calories that are actually consumed in a typical binge.

A NOTE FOR THOSE WHOSE WEIGHT IS RELATIVELY LOW

Although weight gain is unlikely, if you now weigh significantly less than your usual stable weight before you had an eating problem, then you may need to gain a few pounds in order to be able to eat normally. Our bodies tend to have a natural weight at which they settle and which they fight to maintain. If you drop below this weight you can usually only stay there by taking in far fewer calories than someone for whom this is a natural weight. To be able to eat normally, i.e. like others of your age and activity level, you will probably need to return to your natural weight.

If you are overweight (usually defined as a BMI greater than 27) you may be particularly concerned about weight gain. However, our experience suggests that this is just as unlikely to happen to you as it is to someone in the normal weight range. While it may be appropriate for you to lose some weight, we do not recommend that you do this while you are trying to overcome your eating disorder. It is usually best to tackle your bulimia nervosa first. If you do wish to lose weight then, once you have recovered, we recommend that you seek professional advice on a sensible reducing diet.

Box 5.5 Some unrealistic goals

- To eat only fruit and vegetables.

- To diet (as I am doing now – no 'bad' foods at all) without bingeing.

- To lose weight (although my weight is well within the normal range).

- To be slimmer than other people.

- To be a size 8.

- To binge for pleasure only.

BEHAVIOURS

Although less obvious, and not necessarily clearly thought through, you may also be afraid that if you stop any of the other food or weight related behaviours that you carry out regularly, you will gain weight. Andrea worried that if she stopped weighing herself several times a day then her weight would increase by several pounds. We were able to reassure her that, in our experience, this was very unlikely to happen. However, these behaviours are important and may be involved in maintaining your eating disorder. We will examine them in more detail in Chapter 14.

An empty life

Another common fear is that recovery will reveal a very empty life. Often, the various problems and symptoms associated with bulimia nervosa occupy lots of time and leave little room for normal activities, or for thoughts and feelings unrelated to food. This means that stopping bingeing and vomiting will probably, in practice, free up a fair amount of time and 'thinking space'. However, most people have no difficulty in filling their time, or in turning their thoughts to other matters, and returning to a normal way of life. Very occasionally, it is not so easy and life seems extremely empty and lonely without bingeing. If this is likely to be a real problem for you, then you will need a strategy to tackle it. We discuss this fear in more detail in the next chapter.

Dealing with distress

Resisting the urge to binge can be uncomfortable, even distressing. However, it is usually not nearly as distressing as people predict. The strategies presented later in the book will help minimise any distress. It is usually overcome rapidly as you binge less often and get used to coping with problems in other ways. However, a very small number of people do experience extreme distress. If this is likely to be a problem for you, then you will need a strategy in place to manage it. We discuss this fear in more detail in the next chapter.

Bingeing and general coping

Quite often people worry that without their bulimia nervosa they will be unable to cope with any problems which may arise. This fear can make it very difficult to give up the eating disorder and may affect motivation to change. Our patients often have this fear. However, as they progress through the programme and complete the exercises, they are usually delighted to discover that they find other more adaptive ways to deal with life's problems and difficulties.

Facts you should know

Bingeing, compensatory behaviours and dieting all have physical consequences; some of these are dangerous. This is particularly true of vomiting. Knowing about the risks may help to encourage you to change. We summarise them below.

Bingeing

Bingeing causes bloating and abdominal discomfort. It may lead to more general digestive problems, including stomach cramps, wind, constipation and diarrhoea. If the distended stomach presses against the diaphragm it may also cause difficulty with breathing. In rare cases, the stomach wall can become so stretched that it tears. This is a serious medical emergency.

Self-induced vomiting

TEETH

Vomiting exposes teeth to acid from the stomach which will erode dental enamel and rot the teeth. The damage to teeth is irreversible, although it will cease once vomiting stops. Repeated vomiting also causes bad breath.

FACE

With repeated vomiting the glands around the mouth that produce saliva, particularly the parotid gland, may swell gradually. The swelling is painless but the face may take on a round, chubby appearance. This is reversible and will gradually diminish as eating habits improve.

THROAT

Inducing vomiting may result in injuries to the back of the throat, which can then get infected. Recurrent sore throats, blistering (as well as mouth ulcers) and hoarseness are common in those who induce vomiting.

STOMACH

Although rare, violent vomiting can lead to tearing and bleeding of the wall of the oesophagus, the tube leading from the mouth to the stomach. This is also a medical emergency. Vomiting repeatedly over several years can also weaken the oesophagal sphincter, the set of muscles at the top of the stomach. If this happens the contents of the stomach may return spontaneously into the mouth, a distressing, uncomfortable and embarrassing experience.

FINGERS

If fingers are used to stimulate vomiting then damage may occur to the knuckles of the hand used. Abrasions may appear, then scars will form.

ELECTROLYTES

Body fluids and electrolytes (chemicals, such as sodium and potassium capable of conducting electricity that are responsible for normal cell functioning) can also be disturbed in a number of different ways by vomiting; some of them are very serious. The most concerning is a low potassium level (hypokalaemia) which can result in heartbeat irregularities. Symptoms include extreme thirst, dizziness, fluid retention (swelling of legs and arms), weakness and lethargy, muscle twitches and spasms. Up to half of those with bulimia nervosa have some fluid and electrolyte disturbance, although the disturbance is usually mild. The effects are reversible and disappear once vomiting stops.

Laxatives and diuretics

Taking laxatives and diuretics can also lead to electrolyte disturbances. People taking either or both, in addition to vomiting regularly, are particularly at risk. Stopping them suddenly may lead to rebound water retention and thus a temporary increase in weight. The effects of laxatives are usually reversible but some, if taken in large doses over long periods of time, can cause permanent damage to the gut wall. In large quantities they can also cause nausea and spontaneous vomiting. Tolerance to laxatives develops quite quickly, so more and more are needed to achieve the same effect. This increases the risk of self-poisoning and serious electrolyte disturbance.

Dieting

Weight cycling or 'yo-yo' dieting is associated with increased mortality, especially death from cardiovascular disease. Dieting, with or without weight loss, can also affect hormones, resulting in irregular or absent menstruation. It can also disturb some of the physiological mechanisms that control eating, for example, diets that limit or avoid carbohydrates fail to take advantage of carbohydrates' natural ability to suppress appetite. Serotonin, a chemical neurotransmitter in the brain, which is thought to play a role in normal eating and in food selection, can also be affected by dieting, particularly in women, and may exaggerate and increase the risk of developing an eating disorder.

Exercise

Excessive exercise can lead to injury and, not infrequently, a compulsion to exercise may mean that injuries are not given adequate time and rest to heal.

Other problems

OSTEOPOROSIS

Although research is limited, preliminary findings suggest that bulimia nervosa may be associated with osteoporosis. Osteoporosis, or loss of bone density, puts people at risk of stress fractures in later life. It is particularly likely to be a problem in those who have reached a very low weight, whose periods have stopped for a long while because of their eating problem, or who have a history of anorexia nervosa. Dieting (see below) in itself can also affect bone density if the diet chosen is deficient in calcium (this is particularly important before age 30 or so), and may contribute to osteoporosis.

EFFECTS ON FERTILITY AND PREGNANCY

Dieting and weight loss can impair fertility, although the effects are generally reversible. Little is known about the effect of bingeing on fertility and pregnancy. The use of vomiting, laxatives and diuretics is more likely to be harmful. Some pregnant women with bulimia nervosa may be at risk of giving birth to underweight babies. Preliminary work also suggests that the miscarriage rate may be higher than normal for women with bulimia nervosa.

A note of caution

We have noticed that there are two common reactions to reading this information. First, people who do not have any physical problems may conclude that they don't have a very serious problem. Alternatively, if people do have some of these problems then they may feel hopeless, convinced that their eating disorder is beyond their control. Neither reaction is helpful. Bulimia nervosa does carry physical risks – you may well develop some of these problems if you carry on – and it is worth acting now, rather than waiting for a serious physical problem to develop. However, if you already have one or more of these problems then it is important to remember that the majority are reversible and it is possible for you to learn to overcome your eating problem.

Summary exercise

Write a brief summary of what you have learned from this chapter; both from the information presented and from the exercises. Also write down how you will put what you have learned into practice. Then, write the essence of your summary and plans on a small index card. Put this in a bag or inside a diary that you usually carry with you and make time, twice a day, to read the card. Look at Box 5.6 for an example of Hannah's completed index card.

Box 5.6 Hannah's completed index card

What I have learned from the information and exercises:

• I didn't quite realise before just how many problems were being caused by my bulimia nervosa. I was very taken aback to find that bulimia nervosa can cause so many physical health problems.

How I will put what I have learned into practice:

• When I am feeling less motivated to change I will get out and read my problem list and remind myself of my goals.

Chapter summary

This chapter has focused on reasons and motivation to change. The following important points were made:

- Problems typically occur in four main categories: bingeing, compensatory behaviours, dieting and obsessive thoughts. There may also be other problems.

- Nearly everyone has some fears about giving up their eating disorder; many of these fears are shared by others.

- Weight gain is the most common fear; other fears include difficulty in filling an empty life and difficulty dealing with distress. Most of these fears turn out to be unfounded.

- Bulimia nervosa is associated with several physical consequences and dangers, some of them potentially very serious.

We made the following suggestions to help encourage you to change:

- Draw up a list of your problems and goals.

- Turn vague goals into specific goals, so that you will be sure when you have reached them.

- Read about common fears associated with change.

- Read about the physical consequences and dangers of bulimia nervosa.

CHAPTER 6

Why Change?

Unless you are very convinced that change is a good idea you will not be fully committed to the programme, and you may be tempted to give up when things get difficult. This chapter suggests some exercises that will help you increase your commitment to change. First, it will ask you to examine the advantages of changing, together with any fears you may have about change. Then, it will help you to assess the extent to which any of the personal and sensitive fears that you may have about change are realistic (or not). Advice on dealing with realistic fears will also be given.

A warning

Two chapters on change may seem excessive and you may be tempted to skip over this one. However, this chapter is just as important as the last one and we strongly advise you to read it and complete all the exercises. Our patients have found it invaluable to review the exercises in this chapter (like those in the last one) when things get difficult. Reminding yourself of why it is a good idea to change, and of your plans to deal with any problems that may result, can be enormously helpful at such times.

Exercise: Advantages of changing and fears about change

This exercise involves listing all the advantages of changing together with any fears you may have about change. Once you have done this we will ask you to examine (and challenge) any fears in more detail, so that they do not get in the way of your commitment to change. Use Worksheet 6.1 for this exercise and follow the steps below to complete it.

Worksheet 6.1 Advantages of changing, fears and responses to fears

Advantages	Fears	Responses to fears

Outcome:

Step 1: Advantages of changing

In the first column of the worksheet, under 'advantages' list all the advantages of changing that you can think of, taking into account all the problems that you identified in your problem list. Remember, solving some of these problems could well turn into one or more advantages of changing. Change could have an impact on many areas of your life. Think about how it might have a positive effect on your health, weight, social life, friendships, career, family and relationships. As well as thinking about immediate benefits, try to think about any medium and long-term benefits. Remember to use what you have learned so far about bulimia nervosa, particularly what you learned in the last chapter about its physical consequences and dangers. Look at Susan's list in Box 6.1 to help you.

Box 6.1 Susan's advantages of changing

- I'll be able to concentrate better and I won't need to spend so long on each task at work.

- My health (e.g. sore hands, sore throat, energy levels) will improve.

- In general, I'll feel more healthy.

- I won't feel humiliated at having to get rid of the vomit.

- I won't be so preoccupied with thoughts of food, weight and shape.

- I won't have to weigh myself several times a day.

- I'll have money to spend on other things – e.g. nights out with friends, buying CDs.

- I'll be able to take part in and enjoy social activities – e.g. playing squash again, going to the social club at work.

- I'll be able to go out to eat.

- There will be less tension with family and friends.

- I will get on better with my housemates – we'll stop having arguments about food disappearing.

- I'll be able to get closer to my family and friends.

- I'll be able to go to night school to help my career.

- I'll have more self-confidence.

Step 2: Fears about changing

Having covered advantages, move onto the second column 'fears'. In this column list all your fears about change considering, as before, all of the problems that you identified in your problem list. Then, as before, consider your health, weight, social life, friendships, career, family and relationships. Ask yourself whether change could have a negative impact on any of these. Finally, as well as immediate fears, consider whether there might be any medium and long-term negative outcomes. One particularly useful question to ask yourself is: 'What will life be like in, say, five years time if I continue to have an eating problem?' Take a look in Box 6.2 at the fears Karen had.

Box 6.2 Karen's fears about change

- I'll gain weight.

- I won't have a way to treat myself.

- I won't be able to cope with difficult situations or problems.

- I'll lose control of my feelings – be overwhelmed by them.

- I won't be able to have time alone.

Step 3: Outcome

Once your list is complete, consider carefully what completing the exercise suggests. Like most people, you may find that the advantages of change considerably outweigh any possible negative outcomes or fears you may have, particularly when you consider the long-term. Write your conclusions at the bottom of the worksheet under 'outcome'. Fiona wrote the following: 'Although I have some fears about what will happen if I stop bingeing and vomiting I am also losing out on many things – relationships, family life, progressing in my job, etc. If I think five years on then life looks very bleak and unrewarding if I don't tackle the problem now. There are lots of advantages to changing. I need to get my priorities right – bulimia nervosa or a life!'

Step 4: Dealing with fears

Like Karen, you have probably identified at least one, if not several, fears about change. It is usually useful to examine these in more detail so that they do not get in the way of your commitment to change. Use the third column on your worksheet to respond to any fears, using the questions in Box 6.3 to challenge them. Write your responses in the third column 'response to fears'. Not all the questions will be relevant to each fear you have identified – choose those that seem most appropriate each time.

Box 6.3 Questions to challenge fears about change

- What would be another way of looking at this?

- Is there any evidence that this is likely to happen?

- Is this a real fear or is it a false fear that the evidence suggests is unfounded?

- Do the possible long-term advantages outweigh this risk, discomfort or problem?

- If this is likely to be a real problem, how could I deal with it?

Mel's fears and her response to them can be seen in Box 6.4.

Box 6.4 Mel's fears and her response to them

Fears	Response to fears
• I won't have any privacy and uninterrupted time.	• There are other ways of getting time alone, e.g. asking David to take Joe out for a few hours at the weekend.
• I won't be able to lose weight.	• If I ate sensibly and listened to my appetite, I wouldn't need to compensate and would discover my true weight and shape. This might be a few pounds more than I am now, but wouldn't that be better in the long term than the misery of continuing to binge and vomit?
• I'll get fat.	• The evidence suggests that this is very unlikely.
• I won't be able to deal with distressing feelings.	• I can learn other ways to deal with feeling distressed.
• Going to the supermarket is a treat – I won't have a way to treat myself.	• There are other ways to treat myself.
• I won't have a way to deal with problems.	• There are other ways to deal with problems. Focusing everything on weight loss as an achievement is shallow.
• It will be difficult/hard work.	• So why always take the easy option? Think of the costs!

Step 5: Revisiting the outcome

Having responded to any fears, look again at your initial conclusions, written at the bottom of the worksheet under 'outcome'. Is there anything else you can add now? If there is, write it down.

Some specific fears about change

In the last exercise you may have identified some very personal and sensitive fears about change. These will usually involve relationships, but they may also involve fear of a very empty life or of intense distress. It may look to you as though these fears, particularly those about relationships, are realistic. In our experience many will not be. However, very occasionally, changing your eating habits might cause huge disruption to your life. For example, women with bulimia nervosa sometimes have partners who place great value on slenderness or physical attractiveness. It can be very difficult to overcome your eating problem and stop worrying about your weight and shape if a partner continues to attach great importance to them.

Linda (whom you will meet below) was frightened that if she gained any weight her partner would leave her. This was a particular problem because she suspected that her natural weight was a few pounds heavier than her current weight. Relationships with others may also be important. Amanda was an identical twin whose eating problems were bound up in a close and intense relationship with her sister. The two were intensely competitive and jealous of each other. One source of competition, jealousy and ill-feeling was the fact that her sister's husband was Amanda's former boyfriend.

Stopping bingeing and vomiting is likely to bring these sorts of problems into the open. They may be difficult to deal with. What should you do if overcoming your eating problem could, in practice, have a major impact on a very personal and sensitive area of your life? Well, you will need to think very carefully before you move on with the programme. You will need to think about whether or not you are ready and willing, at the moment, to deal with the problems that may result. However, when reaching a decision, take into account not only the difficulties that you may face, but the overall advantages of change that you have identified. Consider too your ability to put into practice plans to deal with the problem. Don't underestimate yourself. When you have an eating disorder it is easy to minimise your strengths and resources.

Exercise: Examining specific fears

It is often useful to try to estimate how realistic any personal and sensitive fears may be. This will help you to be clearer about what stopping binge eating will mean or achieve in practice. After doing this you will have an idea of whether you need to prepare a detailed plan to deal with any problems that may result (advice on this follows later). The following exercise will help you with this. Use Worksheet 6.2 to complete it and follow the steps outlined below.

Worksheet 6.2 Examining specific (personal and sensitive) fears

What you predict will happen:

How likely is it that this will happen (0–100%)?

Evidence for:	Evidence against:

Outcome: How likely do you think it is now that this will happen (0–100%)?

Conclusion:

Step 1: Prediction

At the top write down any very personal and sensitive fears that you have about changing. Write what you predict will happen, particularly in your close relationships, if you overcome your eating problem. Be as specific as possible and make sure you write what you think is the very worst that might happen.

Step 2: Rating

Underneath, rate how likely you think it is that the worst will actually happen using a scale from 0 to 100%, with 0 being 'not at all likely' and 100 being 'extremely likely'.

Step 3: Evidence for

Move onto the left-hand column, labelled 'evidence for'. In this column list all the evidence you have that your fear is realistic, in other words, that is likely to come true in practice.

Step 4: Evidence against

Next, in the right hand column, labelled 'evidence against', list all the evidence which suggests that your fear may not be realistic. Take care if you think others are only interested in your weight and appearance. You may be making the mistake of assuming they attach as much importance to them as you do. Take care too if you are feeling quite depressed. Depression may lead you to focus simply on a negative outcome. For example, a fear of isolation and emptiness if you stop bingeing might easily lead you to forget about the friends you do have.

Box 6.5 Questions to assess the evidence for specific fears

- What makes me think this?

- Am I basing this judgement on one isolated incident?

- Has there been a time when I've thought this and it turned out not to be true?

- Am I focusing simply on a negative outcome because I am feeling generally down?

- Am I ignoring the positives?

- What would my best friend say about this?

- Are others really as concerned about my weight and shape as I am?

You may find it useful to ask yourself the questions in Box 6.5 to help you assess the evidence. As before, not all the questions will be relevant to each fear. Choose those that are most helpful in each case.

Box 6.6 Linda's exercise to examine specific fears

What you predict will happen: If I gain weight (recover) my partner will leave me. I will be criticised for my appearance. He will find me unattractive and won't be interested in sex. He will look at other women more than usual.

The worst thing: He will leave me for someone else.

How likely is it that this will happen (0–100%)? 95%

Evidence for:	Evidence against:
• He frequently says fat women are repulsive and that he could never go out with one. • Every time I have gained a little weight he grabs my flesh and calls me little piggy. • He compares me to other women and says he would like me if I were like them (no hips and large breasts). • When his ex-wife was pregnant he said she was disgusting and he slept around with other women. He has a history of affairs.	• He has a kind side to his character; he is very caring when I'm ill. • He appreciates my company and my sense of humour. • It's not all criticism; there are compliments at times (though mainly about my cooking).

Outcome: How likely do you think it is now that this will happen (0–100%)? 65%

Conclusion: This makes me question what I am doing seeing a man who can be so mean and cruel to me. Staying with him means always having to diet. It may mean always having bulimia nervosa. What kind of a life is this? I want to like myself for who I am, and not how I look. I don't want to worry about my weight and shape anymore. I need to learn to value myself for who I am not for how I look. If others like me that's a bonus. I am going to put myself first and have a go at this programme. Then I can make some decisions about my future.

Step 5: Outcome

Once you have completed this task ask yourself what, on balance, does the evidence suggest? How realistic does your fear seem now? To get a more concrete idea, re-rate it on the 0 to 100% scale. Write your rating at the bottom of the worksheet, under 'outcome'. Then write a summary of your conclusions.

Linda knew, deep down, that she would have to gain a few pounds to reach her stable weight. She was very certain that if this happened her partner would leave her; indeed, she believed it 95%. After completing the exercise she was rather less sure that it would actually happen, but still convinced enough, 65%, to make her question what she was doing in the relationship. In Box 6.6 you can see her completed worksheet.

Managing realistic fears

If, like Linda, this exercise suggests that one or more of your personal and sensitive fears may well be realistic then you will need to think carefully about change. Our experience suggests that it is not usually a good idea to try to deal with too many major problems at once. It is often better to deal with the eating problem first. As you can see in Box 6.6 this is what Linda decided to do. Once your eating has improved then you will feel stronger and more able to deal with any other problems. For most relationship fears this is probably the best strategy.

However, there are some things that you can do in advance. For example, you can flesh out your response to the question in Box 6.3 'How could I deal with this problem?' until you are satisfied that you have a useful and workable plan in hand for when it is needed later on. This will give you confidence in your ability to deal with the problem, as well as something to aim for once your eating problem is resolved. Linda wasn't sure what she wanted to do about her relationship – it didn't look good – but she took our advice and worked on her eating problem before making any major decisions about it. As she did so she began to make plans for how she would deal with this problem once her eating had improved.

Relationship problems

If the problem is a relationship then it might be useful to discuss the implications of change, insofar as you can foresee them, with your partner or family member. This will help you gauge their likely reaction. You may be pleasantly surprised to discover that they are prepared to support you while you change, and willing to renegotiate aspects of your relationship once you have overcome your eating problem.

Isolation and an empty life

If the problem is extreme isolation and a very empty life then, unlike many other personal and sensitive issues, it is usually helpful to start work on this as soon as possible. If the space is not filled quickly with interesting and enjoyable things, then you will be tempted to go back to bingeing. Sharon followed the plan in Box 6.7 to help her fill up the space that would be left by not bingeing.

Box 6.7 A plan to deal with loneliness and isolation

Step 1: Make a list of all the activities, interests and friendships that you no longer participate in because of bulimia nervosa.

Step 2: Reflect and record how you would like to spend your time, if not spending so much time on bingeing and on worrying about food and about your weight and shape.

Step 3: Plan an enjoyable activity (the easiest first) that you have given up. Arrange to do it (on the day of the week and at the time that seems easiest).

Step 4: Review what you did – ask 'what did I learn from this?'

Step 5: Gradually plan more activities, reviewing each one along the way. Do the same for interests and for getting in touch with old friends.

Discomfort when stopping bingeing

Some people feel temporarily more distressed and emotionally uncomfortable when they reduce or stop bingeing. These feelings usually decrease given a little time. However, to speed things up as your eating improves, you can implement a plan to deal with your feelings as soon as you start work on your eating. Again, ask yourself 'How could I deal with this?', and draw up a detailed plan to help you manage your distress (you may already have begun to do this in the last exercise). Remember, if you stick with it and devise effective ways to manage it, your distress will ultimately lessen.

Carol followed the plan in Box 6.8 to deal with the distress she experienced when trying to stop bingeing. At first she found it difficult to think of more than one or two ways to soothe herself apart from bingeing. Eventually however, she developed a long list. This included listening to calming music, having a long hot bath, walking in the sunshine, buying cards for friends and cuddling the cat. When she felt very upset, her strategies included getting out a teddy bear that her partner had given her, or wrapping herself in a large blanket with a hot water bottle.

Box 6.8 A plan to deal with distress

Step 1:   Be prepared. Make a list of soothing things you can do to be nicer to yourself that don't involve food. Do this at a time when you are not feeling distressed.

Step 2:   Keep the list with you at all times.

Step 3:   When (and preferably before) distress increases, select an activity from the list.

Step 4:   Try out the activity.

Step 5:   Afterwards, reflect and review. Did it help? If not, why not? What could you do differently next time?

Step 6:   Add to and expand your list in the light of your review.

Summary exercise

Write a brief summary of what you have learned from this chapter, both from the information presented and from the exercises. Also write down how you will put what you have learned into practice. Then, write the essence of your summary and plans on a small index card. Put this in a bag or inside a diary that you usually carry with you and make time, twice a day, to read the card.

Chapter summary

This chapter has helped you increase your commitment to change. The following important points were made:

- The advantages of change will outweigh any possible negative outcomes or fears.

- Some specific fears may be very personal and sensitive.

- Although many specific (sensitive and personal) fears are often unfounded, some may be realistic.

- It is usually best to put specific, realistic fears on hold until your eating has improved.

- If there is a real possibility that you will find it very difficult to fill the space made by not bingeing, or if you are likely to become distressed, make plans to deal with these early on.

We made the following suggestions to help you increase your commitment to change:

- Examine the advantages of changing and your fears about change.

- Identify any specific (personal and sensitive) fears.

- Examine how realistic specific fears are.

- Make plans to deal with realistic fears, in so far as is possible at this stage, remembering that it is best to tackle most of them once you have stopped bingeing and vomiting and are feeling stronger.

CHAPTER 7

The Cognitive Model

Cognitive theory is the model on which our programme is based. We introduced it briefly in Chapter 4, where we told you how thoughts, feelings and behaviour in bulimia nervosa are linked in vicious circles. We also explained that interrupting them will enable you to overcome your eating problem (more on this later). However, before you can learn how to do this you need to know how to identify examples of your own vicious circles. To assist you, this chapter will introduce you to some typical examples taken from our clinical work. It will then help you to identify the vicious circle that keeps your own binge eating going. First, however, we will introduce you to an A-B-C analysis.

The A-B-C analysis

The A-B-C analysis forms the basis of the vicious circles we will discuss later in the chapter. A-B-C describes the link between activating events, thoughts and consequences. As are the activating event or triggers of distress. These can be situations or initial thoughts. Bs are the bad or negative thoughts that result. Cs are the consequences of the thoughts. Consequences include both emotions (or feelings) and behaviours.

Exercise: Identifying As, Bs and Cs

It is not always easy to identify As, Bs and Cs at first, you may need to practise with several examples. Below we present an exercise that will help you identify them and, importantly, distinguish between them, using situations based on your own experience. Use Worksheet 7.1 and follow the step-by-step instructions below.

Worksheet 7.1 An A-B-C analysis

As or activating events	Bs or thoughts	Cs or consequences

Step 1: Identifying activating events or As

First of all you need to identify a recent, specific situation in which you felt upset or distressed, and that eventually resulted in bingeing and vomiting. To help you do this, ask yourself the questions in Box 7.1 and record your answers under the As column on your worksheet.

Box 7.1 Identifying activating events or As

- When was it?

- Where were you?

- Who were you with?

- What were you doing?

- What were you thinking about?

After asking yourself these questions, you should have a detailed description of an activating event. Charlie described one of the situations which led to a binge as follows: 'It was yesterday. I was in the sitting room by myself, watching TV and eating crumpets. I was thinking of Easter Sunday and what a difficult day it would be with all that food around. I was thinking it will probably all go disastrously wrong. I was thinking that I'd probably binge.' Once you have identified the activating events or As, move on to identify your thoughts or Bs.

Step 2: Identifying thoughts or Bs

To help you identify your thoughts or Bs, ask yourself the questions in Box 7.2. Record your answers under the Bs column on your worksheet. Thoughts about yourself are particularly important in eating disorders; make sure that you take care to identify any of these.

You will see that we have also included questions about images or pictures. These are common in activating events and usually contain one or more thoughts. If you do have an image or picture, remember to ask yourself the two questions about images. You should now have a description of what went through your mind (your thoughts) in the activating event. Thoughts arise in and from the activating event. Draw in an arrow from the As to the Bs to link them in this way.

Charlie described her thoughts as follows: 'I might as well just binge now and get it out of the way; I can't control my eating.' She also had an image of herself on Easter Day, eating and eating until she ballooned into a huge, wobbly bubble. The thoughts in her image were similar to those she had already identified: 'I lack control over my eating.'

Box 7.2 Identifying thoughts or Bs

- What was running through your mind in the activating event?

- What were you saying to yourself?

- Were there any images or pictures? What were the thoughts in the images?

- What were you thinking about yourself?

Step 3: Identifying consequences or C's

Concentrate on the feelings or emotions that resulted from your thoughts or Bs. Ask yourself the questions in Box 7.3 and write your answers under the Cs column of your worksheet.

Box 7.3 Identifying consequences or Cs

- What feelings did you have?

- What did you do?

Feelings and behaviours result from your bad thoughts or Bs. Draw in a second arrow from your Bs to your Cs to show this link. You now have an A-B-C analysis. Charlie's Cs or consequences were feelings of anxiety. She then started to eat more, and eating two crumpets turned into a binge. Charlie's activating event was food related. However, many activating events are apparently unrelated to food, or to weight and shape.

Take a look at one of Susannah's A-B-C analyses, in Box 7.4. This illustrates how a situation apparently unrelated to food and eating, weight and shape can result in a binge.

Box 7.4 Susannah's A-B-C analysis

As or activating events	Bs or thoughts	Cs or consequences
This afternoon, at work, alone, in my office, thinking about a disagreement with a colleague about the sales ledger. Felt upset, muddled, confused.	I feel out of control – my thoughts and feelings are all over the place – it's going to get worse and worse if I don't do something about it. I can't bear it any longer – bingeing will take away these bad feelings.	Felt worried and anxious. Started eating a sandwich from the vending machine, then left work early to binge.

A note about thoughts and feelings

It is sometimes difficult, at first, to distinguish between thoughts and feelings. It is important to do so because of the key role thoughts have in bringing about change in cognitive therapy. The difficulty usually arises because we often use the words 'I feel' to describe a thought. For example, we say 'I feel stupid, I feel useless.' Feelings are emotions, for example, anger, sadness, anxiety, depression, panic, guilt, while thoughts are the things you tell yourself, for example, 'I'm no good, I'm bad, I'm a failure, I've no self-control.' This distinction is important when we come to challenge thoughts: feelings are just feelings; they can't be challenged or changed in the same way. In cognitive therapy it is challenging the thoughts that will change your feelings and stop you bingeing and vomiting. If you are struggling to identify and distinguish between thoughts and feelings, the exercise in Appendix 3 (p.230–1) might be helpful before you carry on with the rest of the programme.

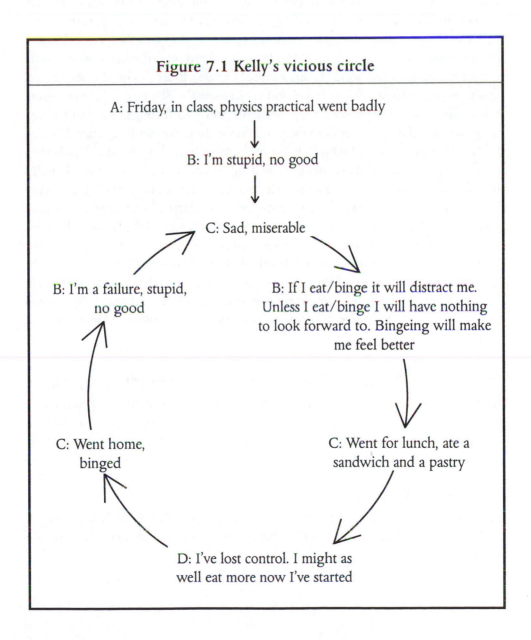

Figure 7.1 Kelly's vicious circle

A: Friday, in class, physics practical went badly

B: I'm stupid, no good

C: Sad, miserable

B: I'm a failure, stupid, no good

B: If I eat/binge it will distract me. Unless I eat/binge I will have nothing to look forward to. Bingeing will make me feel better

C: Went home, binged

C: Went for lunch, ate a sandwich and a pastry

D: I've lost control. I might as well eat more now I've started

How A-B-C becomes a vicious circle

Now that you have conducted an A-B-C analysis we will show you how A-B-C turns into a vicious circle. So far we have shown you how As lead to Bs which, in turn, lead to Cs. However Bs and Cs also link together to form vicious circles (see Chapter 5). Together they create a downward spiral of thoughts, feelings and behaviours that keep bulimia nervosa going. An example of how this tends to work for bingeing can be seen in Figure 7.1. This is one of Kelly's vicious circles. As you can see, the A-B-C analysis provides a way into her vicious circle. Then Bs and Cs alternate, creating a vicious cycle. We will talk you through Kelly's vicious circle. Kelly was a first year science student at college. That morning, a Friday, she had been in class carrying out a practical experiment. She had made one or two mistakes and the practical hadn't quite turned out as she had hoped. Her thoughts about herself when it went wrong were 'I'm stupid, I'm no good.' Understandably, having these thoughts made her feel upset. In particular she felt very sad and very miserable. She began to think about eating as a way to cope with these thoughts and bad feelings. She felt eating/bingeing would distract her from them, that it would make her feel better. She also had the thought, 'Unless I binge, I will have nothing to look forward to.' Kelly then went for lunch, with all these thoughts buzzing around in her head. At lunch with a friend she ate a sandwich and a pastry. This made her feel out of control and she then had the thought, 'I might as well eat more now I've started.' As a result, instead of going to the library to start on her essay as she had originally planned, she went home and binged. However, as you can see from her vicious circle, this only made her think that she was stupid and no good again. In fact, she was back exactly where she had started out – feeling bad about herself and thinking bad thoughts about herself. Indeed, if anything, she felt even worse than she had before she binged. As you will know only too well, despite the consequences, this circle is powerful and not at all easy to break.

Exercise: Identifying the vicious circle that maintains your bingeing

In this exercise we will show you how your own A-B-C example can turn into a vicious circle of thoughts, feelings and behaviours. Use Worksheet 7.2, following the step by step instructions below. The aim is for you to be able to identify your own vicious circles.

Step 1: The A-B-C analysis

Fill in the A-B-C section at the top using the example your A-B-C analysis produced, or if you prefer, repeat it with a new example, using the questions in the last exercise to help you.

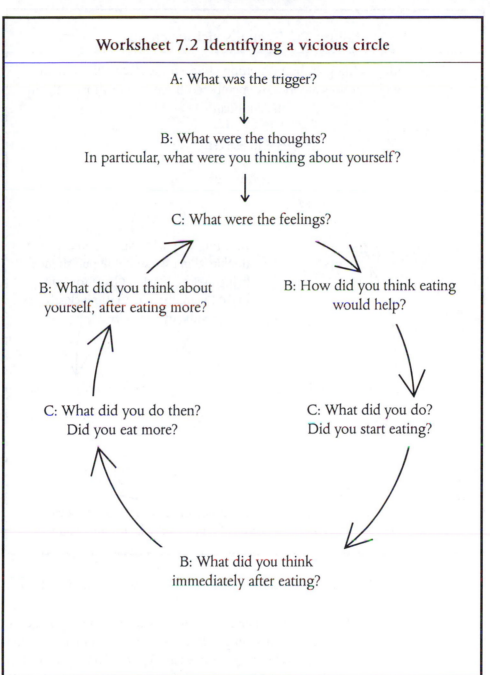

Worksheet 7.2 Identifying a vicious circle

A: What was the trigger?

B: What were the thoughts?
In particular, what were you thinking about yourself?

C: What were the feelings?

B: What did you think about yourself, after eating more?

B: How did you think eating would help?

C: What did you do then? Did you eat more?

C: What did you do? Did you start eating?

B: What did you think immediately after eating?

Step 2: The vicious circle

Ask yourself the questions on the worksheet in sequence, following the arrows, to identify what keeps your eating problem alive. Write your answers in the spaces provided. Notice that your circle consists of a series of A-B-C-B-Cs where bad

Figure 7.2 Rachel's vicious circle

A: Yesterday evening, at home, getting children's tea. Dwelling on an argument with my boss at work. Remembered there was birthday cake in the cupboard.

↓

B: I'm useless.

↓

C: Anxious.

B: I'm ugly, lazy, disgusting, useless.

B: Eating will help with the anxiety and thinking I'm useless; it will punish me for being useless. If I don't have something to eat I won't be able to think clearly or get on with anything else.

C: Ate more and more cake/binged.

C: Ate small piece of cake.

B: I've got to eat more. The bad side of my character has taken over. I can't control my eating. I'll make myself sick afterwards.

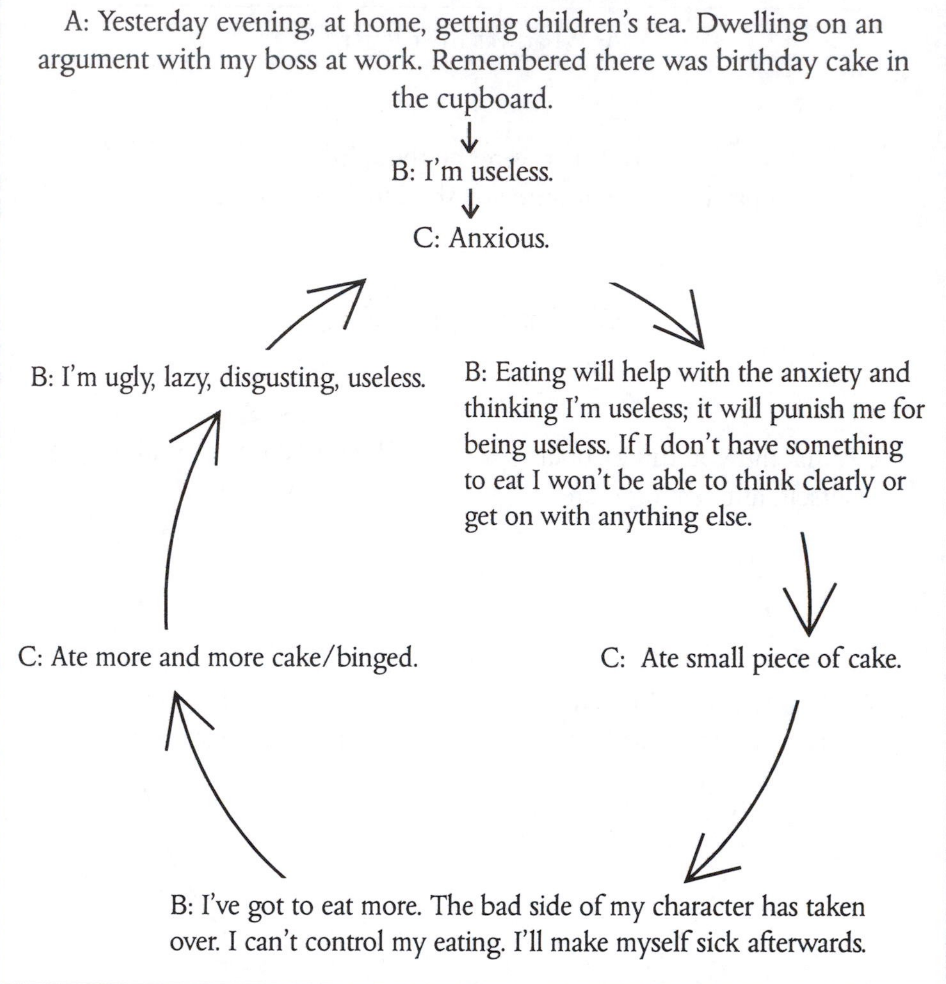

thoughts (B) are followed by consequences (C) which may be followed by further bad thoughts (B) and so on.

You should now be beginning to get an idea of what keeps your bingeing going on a moment by moment basis. Notice, in particular, the thoughts or Bs. In later chapters we will teach you how to challenge these. Identifying the thoughts or Bs is not always easy. Don't be discouraged if you found the last exercise hard. To help you, take a look at Rachel's vicious circle in Figure 7.2. This is what she discovered when she did this exercise. If necessary, practice doing the vicious circle exercise again. You may need to go through it several times, using examples of different times when you binged and vomited until you are confident in your ability to identify thoughts.

In Figure 7.2 you can see one of Rachel's vicious circles. We will take you slowly through it so that you can see how the thoughts or Bs, feelings and behaviour or Cs fit together and result in bingeing.

For Rachel, the trigger or A was an argument at work with her boss. The argument left her thinking badly about herself. As she dwelt on the argument, she had the thought about herself, or B, 'I'm useless.' This thought made her feel very anxious, a C. Soon she found herself thinking that eating would help with (take away) the anxiety and the thought that she was useless. Bingeing would also punish her for being so useless. She had the thought, 'If I don't have something to eat I won't be able to think clearly or get on with anything else.' The result was that she ate a small piece of cake. She then had the following thoughts 'I've got to eat more', 'the bad side of my character has taken over', 'I can't control my eating,' and 'I'll make myself sick afterwards'. As a result she ate more of the cake.

As you can see in Figure 7.2 it led, in the end, to a binge (more cake followed by lots of buttered toast), in a repeated attempt to deal with the thoughts and feelings, as the vicious circle gathered speed and spiralled downwards into a binge. However, eating and ultimately bingeing only made her feel worse about herself. She had several distressing thoughts, including the thought 'I'm useless' once more. This completed her vicious circle. This detailed slow motion rerun of bingeing is important in cognitive therapy. It is particularly helpful in identifying the thoughts that keep bingeing going. Interrupting your own vicious circles is going to depend on being able to identify these.

A note about vomiting

This can also be included in the vicious circle. See Figure 7.3 for an example of a vicious circle (with the activating event or A summarised) including vomiting.

In brief, vomiting acts as a 'safety' behaviour. It keeps you safe from gaining weight. It is important; in this example, bingeing leads to the thoughts 'I'll get fat' and 'I can't bear to feel so bad, I can't deal with this distress.' Vomiting then occurs, both to prevent weight gain and to deal with the distress caused by bingeing. Like bingeing, vomiting is an unhelpful long term coping strategy, i.e. a way to deal with negative thoughts and distressing feelings. Like bingeing it leads to further negative thoughts, especially negative thoughts about yourself. In this example, it reinforces the thought 'I'm a failure'. Thus it makes further bingeing (and therefore further vomiting) more likely. Although important, our clinical experience suggests that once the bingeing vicious circle has been broken and bingeing stops, then vomiting stops as well. We think this is because, in part, our programme tackles bingeing as an unhelpful coping strategy. Once alternative coping strategies are discovered, you will have other ways to cope with distress and will not need to resort to either bingeing or vomiting any more. Because of this strong link between the two, our programme will focus primarily on bingeing rather than on vomiting (or other compensatory behaviours).

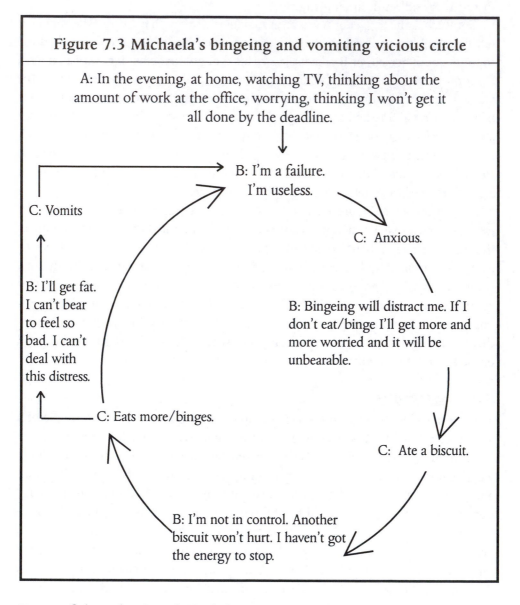

Figure 7.3 Michaela's bingeing and vomiting vicious circle

A: In the evening, at home, watching TV, thinking about the amount of work at the office, worrying, thinking I won't get it all done by the deadline.

B: I'm a failure. I'm useless.

C: Vomits

C: Anxious.

B: I'll get fat. I can't bear to feel so bad. I can't deal with this distress.

B: Bingeing will distract me. If I don't eat/binge I'll get more and more worried and it will be unbearable.

C: Eats more/binges.

C: Ate a biscuit.

B: I'm not in control. Another biscuit won't hurt. I haven't got the energy to stop.

Types of thought: A technical note

As you will discover later, there are several different types of thought. Within the vicious circle they are all linked together. Positive beliefs about eating develop as a way to cope with low self-esteem and distress (e.g. 'eating will make me feel better about myself'). At the same time fear of getting fat develops (e.g. 'if I go ahead and eat that sandwich I'll get fat/distressed/feel I've failed'). Again, eating (or not eating) is being used to cope with feelings and low self-esteem. The dissonance or tension between these two beliefs is resolved, once eating has started, by permissive thoughts (e.g. 'what the hell, I might as well eat a bit more now I've started'). Finally, the guilt that results from bingeing is resolved by believing that the person has no control over her eating. In later chapters we will focus on thoughts of no control, permissive thoughts and positive beliefs about eating as well as fears about eating.

Chapter summary

This chapter has provided you with detailed information on the cognitive model. The following important points were made:

- As are activating events, Bs are bad thoughts, Cs are consequences (feelings and behaviours).
- The A-B-C relationship forms the basis of the vicious circles that maintain your eating disorder.
- It is important to distinguish between thoughts and feelings.
- Thoughts or Bs link with Cs or consequences to create a downward spiral that keeps bingeing going.
- It may take a little practice to identify bad thoughts or Bs.
- There are several types of thought: thoughts of no control, permissive thoughts and positive beliefs about eating are particularly important, together with fears about eating.

The following suggestions were made to help you apply the model to your own eating behaviour:

- Use the questions provided to produce an A-B-C analysis.
- Building on your A-B-C analysis, identify one of the typical vicious circles that keeps your bingeing going.
- If you find thoughts or Bs hard to identify, practise identifying vicious circles several times.

CHAPTER 8

The Myth of Control

As you discovered in the last chapter, negative thoughts are important in the bingeing vicious circle, and help to maintain bingeing. Although there is more than one type of negative thought, our experience suggests that thoughts of no control are crucial. In this chapter we will show you some examples of thoughts of no control. Next, we will help you identify what keeps your belief in lack of control going; in other words, what evidence you have that it is true. We will then ask you to investigate whether it is possible that you might be mistaken about having no control.

Before you read on

It can be difficult to give up thoughts that you lack control over your eating. After all, there are likely to be some advantages to holding onto them. For example, it will often 'let you off the hook.' Shona told herself 'My eating is out of control; it's not my fault, I can't help it.' Part of getting better is to 'own your own problem'; accept that you have some responsibility for what you do.

Too much control

You may be surprised to hear that, paradoxically, the problem is not that people with bulimia nervosa lack control; on the contrary, the problem is often that they are exercising too much control. Constant dieting, avoiding certain foods, refusing food at parties, etc. requires lots of hard work and considerable control.

Thoughts of no control

Examples of thoughts of no control, i.e. that you can't control your eating, can be seen in Box 8.1.

Box 8.1 Thoughts of no control: Some examples

- I'm out of control.

- I can't stop myself.

- I've no self willpower.

- I can't help it.

- I can't control my eating.

Evidence for no control

If you believe that you can't control your eating, then you will have good reasons (evidence) for thinking this. Dawn came up with several pieces of evidence. These included: eating chocolate, puddings and other 'banned' items; believing that bingeing was 'automatic' and didn't involve thinking; and having other people say 'it's not your fault, you can't help it'. Later in this chapter we will show you how to identify the evidence you have, in your own case. First, however, we will discuss three common types of evidence that people with bulimia nervosa often use to support the belief that they can't control their eating.

Bingeing 'all the time'

It may feel as though you are bingeing all or most of the time. This is never strictly speaking true (no one binges 24 hours a day). However, the feeling that it is true is often taken as evidence that it is a fact. Denise had three binges in one afternoon. By bedtime she was exhausted and very depressed. It felt as though she had spent the whole day bingeing. Although she had had a relatively normal morning – taking her oldest child to school and the youngest to a mother and toddler group – she found herself thinking 'I've spent all day bingeing; I binge all the time', even though this was not true.

Eating small or normal amounts

Eating a small or relatively normal amount of food may make you think that you have lost control. Eating such amounts may be used as evidence for lack of control, even though you would not think that a friend eating a similar amount had lost control. Karina didn't usually eat lunch and when she had a sandwich with a colleague from work one day she felt extremely guilty. She thought 'this just goes to show that I can't control myself around food'. She was completely ignoring the fact that she usually successfully ate nothing at lunchtime.

Sensations of fullness and hunger

One very common type of evidence involves bodily sensations, particularly feeling full after eating or feeling hungry. People with bulimia nervosa tend to monitor sensations of fullness and hunger very closely. Having these sensations is in itself often taken as evidence of lack of control over eating. When they are interpreted in this way, sensations of fullness and hunger can trigger off a binge. This is a very quick way into a binge. Carla felt full and bloated round her stomach after eating a normal meal with her family. She took the fullness and bloated feeling as a sign that she was getting fat and, crucially, that she had lost control, when these were just normal feelings that everyone experiences at times.

Exercise: Identifying the evidence for lack of control

This exercise will help you to identify precisely what it is that makes you think you can't control your own eating. Use Worksheet 8.1 for this exercise and follow the step- by-step instructions below.

Step 1: Lack of control thoughts

At the top of the worksheet write down one or more typical examples of your lack of control thoughts, using your own words and, as far as possible, the words that you say to yourself in the middle of a binge. You may find it helpful to ask yourself, 'What does this say about my sense of control?'

Step 2: Belief in each

Rate how much you believe each thought on a scale from 0–100%, with 0 being 'I don't believe this thought at all' and 100 being 'I am completely convinced that this thought is true'.

Step 3: Evidence for

Next, in the left-hand column 'evidence for' make a list of all the things that make you think that you can't control your eating. Consider the three different categories of evidence discussed above (bingeing all the time, eating small or normal amounts, sensations of hunger and fullness) to see whether or not you could be using evidence that falls into each of these categories. However, make sure you include all your evidence, even if it does not fall into these categories.

To help you, take a look in Box 8.2 at the evidence Gwen was using to support her beliefs that she lacked control. Besides evidence related to 'bingeing all the time' and eating small or normal amounts (such as lunch), she had quite a few other pieces of evidence too.

Worksheet 8.1 Evidence for and against lack of control over eating

Lack of control thoughts:	Belief in each (0–100%):

Evidence for	Evidence against

Outcome:

Re-rate belief in each thought (0–100%):

Box: 8.2 Gwen's evidence for lack of control over her eating

- Bingeing 'all the time'.

- Eating lunch.

- Starting bingeing in the first place.

- Not being able to stop at the right amount of food.

- Eating chocolate and sweets.

- Having no willpower (in general).

- Not being able to control my eating all the time, 24 hours a day.

Reinterpreting the evidence for lack of control

You have now identified the evidence that makes you think that you can't control your eating. The next step is to examine this evidence more carefully. Research suggests that people with bulimia nervosa often misinterpret (usually in a negative direction) events or situations that concern food and eating, weight and shape. If you have bulimia nervosa then it is quite likely that you do this too. In particular, you may be misinterpreting the evidence relevant to your belief that you can't control your eating. There are four ways in which you may be doing this. They are:

- catastrophising (making negative predictions without considering other possible outcomes);
- selective attention (focusing on one aspect of the problem while discounting or ignoring others);
- emotional reasoning (being misled by how you feel and thinking that feelings are facts);
- double standards (having one rule or standard for yourself and another for everyone else). All four can lead you to the wrong conclusion about control. You can read examples of all four types of reasoning below.

Catastrophising

Victoria believed that if she ate a small amount she had lost control. After eating one biscuit with her coffee she thought 'my eating is completely out of control'.

Selective attention

Sophie ate one square of chocolate at 5 pm. It was the first thing she had eaten all day. She had the thought 'I just can't control my eating'. She focused on the fact that she had eaten one thing and ignored the fact that she had not eaten anything else all day. This (selective attention) reinforced her thought that she lacked control.

Emotional reasoning

Lydia believed that feeling full after eating a small amount of food was evidence that she had lost control. She had the thought 'if I feel bloated and fat, it means I lack control over my eating'.

Double standards

Susie ate a packet of crisps one morning, as did a colleague, in her coffee break at work. She thought to herself 'that just shows I can't control my eating', even though she didn't think the same about her colleague.

We have devised some questions that, as part of the next exercise, will help you to challenge these four distorted ways of thinking. The aim of this exercise is to see whether there is another way to look at the evidence; in particular, a way that is inconsistent with the belief that you can't control your eating. The questions can be seen in *Box 8.3*.

Box 8.3 Questions to challenge evidence for lack of control

Catastrophisation: Am I blowing things up out of all proportion? Am I making a mountain out of a molehill?

Selective attention: Is this true 100% of the time? Do I have any evidence which shows that this is not true all the time?

Emotional reasoning: Am I being misled by how I feel instead of focusing on the facts? Is there another way to look at this? Is there another explanation for this (for example, for feeling full after eating) other than loss of control?

Double standards: What would I say to someone else, for example, my best friend? Would I tell them that eating a relatively small or normal amount of food is equivalent to losing control? How would I define loss of control for someone else?

Exercise: Reinterpreting the evidence for lack of control

This exercise will help you to challenge and reinterpret the evidence you have found. Go back to Worksheet 8.1 and follow the step-by-step instructions below.

Step 1: Evidence against

In the right-hand column of the worksheet, 'evidence against', write your responses, using the questions in Box 8.3, to challenge the evidence that you found in support of the belief that you lack control. Challenge and reinterpret one piece of evidence at a time.

Step 2: Outcome

When you have worked your way through all the evidence, consider what the evidence now suggests, on balance, and write a brief summary of your conclusions under 'outcome' near the bottom of your worksheet.

Step 3: Re-rate beliefs

Below 'outcome', re-rate your initial thoughts using the same 0–100% rating scale as before.

Take a look in Box 8.4 at Mary's evidence for and against her lack of control thoughts, and the outcome of the exercise for her, to help you.

Qualifications: 'yes, but' thoughts

The doubt that you can control your eating usually remains because there are some qualifications to the new belief that you do, in fact, have some control over your eating. These qualifications are often expressed in the form of 'yes, but' thoughts. For example, Ruth said: 'Yes, I know I can control my eating sometimes, for example, when I'm with a friend or when I'm at work, but I can't control it at home in the evenings, I just have to binge.'

A mini exercise

If you still believe that you don't have much control over your eating, ask yourself whether you have any 'yes, but' thoughts about the evidence you generated against your belief on Worksheet 8.1. Ask yourself the same questions that we asked Ruth: 'How is it that you binge in some situations but not others; what makes the difference, in particular, what thoughts make it easy to binge?' Then ask yourself what this tells you about whether or not you do have control and whether (for very good reasons, like permissive self-talk) you are making a choice to binge or not, depending on the situation.

Box 8.4 Mary's evidence for and against her lack of control thoughts

Lack of control thoughts:	Belief in each (0–100%):
• I'm not in control	100%
• I can't control what or how much food I eat	100%

Evidence for	Evidence against
• Once I start eating I can't stop.	• I don't lose control when other people are around, I can eat small amounts then and stop.
• If food is there I have to eat it – I can't help myself.	• That's not so, just because it's there doesn't mean its compulsory for me to eat it. I can stop myself. I have got some control over food. For example, I can eat biscuits sometimes and not binge (e.g. at work). I wouldn't binge if a friend came round. I don't binge all the time, i.e. 24 hours a day.
• I eat chocolate (and other high calorie foods) sometimes.	• Sometimes I have a bar of chocolate in the 'fridge for over a week; eating one small bar of chocolate isn't the same as losing control, it's normal eating.
• I'm just not in control of my life – losing control of my eating is just one example of this.	• I've made some important decisions about my future recently – that's taking control of what will happen to me. Maybe I can do the same for my eating.

Outcome: I do have some control over my eating. In particular, I have a choice whether to binge or not. Don't let it get the better of you. Stick with it.

Re-rate belief in each thought, 0–100%:

I'm not in control 20%.

I can't control what or how much food I eat 30%.

Chapter summary

This chapter has focused on the thought that you can't control your eating. The following important points were made:

- In the bingeing vicious circle thoughts of no control are particularly crucial.

- You have good reason (evidence) to think that you can't control your eating.

- Three common types of evidence for loss of control involve thinking that you binge 'all the time', eating small or normal amounts of food, and experiencing sensations of hunger and fullness.

- Although you have evidence that you lack control you may be misinterpreting the evidence.

- Common misinterpretations of the evidence involve catastrophisation, selective attention, emotional reasoning and double standards.

- You need to realise that you do have some degree of control and that you choose to binge or not to binge.

We made the following suggestions to help you identify the evidence you are using to support the belief that you can't control your eating and, most importantly, to build up your sense of control:

- Identify what makes you think you can't control your eating.

- Reinterpret the evidence using a series of questions.

- Deal with any 'yes, but' thoughts that may still be keeping the belief in no control alive.

- Develop a sense of choice.

CHAPTER 9

Confirming Control

This chapter continues to address any remaining thoughts that you have little or no control over your eating. In it, we will suggest ways in which you can act, rather like a scientist, to confirm and build up a sense of control over your eating.

Some people find that this happens relatively quickly (one or two experiments is enough), others find that it takes longer. Don't be discouraged if it takes longer than you expect (or if you have setbacks along the way). Remember what we said in Chapter 1, as long as you are making progress, no matter how slowly, then you will almost certainly get there in the end. Try to keep this in mind as you work through the book.

Confirming control: Behavioural experiments

Challenging your lack of control thoughts and dealing with any 'yes but' thoughts will have given you some confidence that you can control your eating. Now you need to work to increase this confidence. Ultimately, you should aim to believe 100 per cent that 'I can control my eating'. To achieve this we suggest that you become a scientist and carry out a series of behavioural experiments. Scientists carry out experiments to test or confirm their hypotheses (their beliefs and ideas). We suggest that you treat your new belief, 'I can control my eating', as an idea or hypothesis and use behavioural experiments to test and confirm it. The aim is to build up your confidence in this belief.

Planning behavioural experiments

Because each person with bulimia nervosa is different and binges in different situations and under different circumstances, you will need to design and carry out the behavioural experiments that are right for you. The experiments should also be graded. This means that you should start with a situation in which you think it will be relatively easy to confirm that you do have control. You should then build up to the more difficult situations in a series of small steps. Eventually you will be able to tackle the most difficult situation.

Charlotte listed all the situations in which she usually binged and rated them each from 0–100% for how difficult it would be not to binge in them, with 0 being 'not at all difficult' and 100 being 'as difficult as I can imagine'. She then planned a series of experiments to confirm her belief that she did have control, starting with the situation in which she would find it easiest not to binge. Having completed the first situation successfully she moved on to the next most difficult situation.

Gradually she worked up her list to the most difficult situation of all. She recorded brief details of each experiment, including the date and time and, most importantly, her belief in the thought 'I can control my eating' right at the start and immediately after completing each experiment.

To help herself take the decision not to binge in each situation she did two further things. First, she drew up a list of the advantages and disadvantages (the pros and the cons) of bingeing in the situation she was working on. Second, she drew up an action plan; a list of things that she could do instead of bingeing, including things that would help her to cope with any distressing feelings.

Ideas for experiments

Below we suggest two experiments that you can carry out to confirm and build up a sense of control over your eating.

Binge postponement

This is a useful strategy to keep in mind, particularly if you are trying to break difficult, risky situations into smaller steps (see below). It simply means what it says; in the difficult situation plan a series of experiments in which bingeing is postponed for increasing lengths of time. Rita tried this to stop herself bingeing on Saturday afternoons, while she was alone at home. If she managed to get to 4 pm without bingeing then she rarely binged after this. She divided 12 noon to 4 pm into half-hour slots. First she planned to reach 12.30 pm without bingeing, then 1 pm, then 1.30 pm until, over the course of several weekends, she reached 4 pm.

Trying to lose control

This can be a powerful strategy. Follow the steps in Box 9.1. You should choose a time when you are usually unlikely to binge and, as the phrase suggests, you should try as hard as possible to make yourself lose control of your eating.

Box 9.1 Trying to lose control

Step 1: Rate how much you believe 'I can control my eating' on a 0–100% scale.

Step 2: Choose a time when you wouldn't usually binge.

Step 3: Put food in front of you.

Step 4: Try and lose control.

Step 5: Record what happened. If you ate the food what did you think just before eating it? If you didn't eat the food what thoughts stopped you?

Step 6: Ask yourself, what have I learned about whether or not I choose to binge? What have I learned about whether or not I have control over my eating?

Step 7: Rate how much you believe 'I can control my eating' again, on the same 0–100% scale.

Exercise: Planning and carrying out behavioural experiments

This exercise will help you to plan and carry out your own behavioural experiments. Use Worksheet 9.1 for this exercise and follow the steps below.

Worksheet 9.1 Hierarchy of difficult situations

Situation	Difficulty (0–100%)	Order

Step 1

Start by identifying all the situations in which you find it difficult not to binge. Make a list of them under 'situation'.

Step 2

Rate each situation, under 'difficulty' on a scale from 0 to 100%, with 0 being 'not at all difficult' and 100 being 'as difficult as I can imagine'. If they all seem equally difficult, particularly if you have rated them all near the top end of the scale, break some into smaller, easier steps, perhaps using the binge postponement strategy. You want to maximise your chances of success so don't make the task impossibly difficult.

Step 3: Order

Having done this, number the situations in ascending order of difficulty, under 'order', from least difficult to most difficult. Lucy's hierarchy of difficult situations can be seen in Box 9.2.

Box 9.2 Lucy's hierarchy of difficult situations

Situation	Difficulty (0–100%)	Order
• Being alone.	100	12
• Being at home, lots of food available, knowing it won't be missed, knowing I can vomit afterwards.	80	9
• Having to disagree with someone more senior at work.	50	4
• Walking past the corner shop.	25	1
• Feeling bored.	65	6
• Lack of structure to my day (more likely to binge at weekends or in the evenings).	85	10
• Loss of willpower, motivation.	90	11
• Feeling upset, unhappy or depressed (e.g. feeling excluded by my friends).	70	7
• Worrying about putting on weight.	60	5
• Having to go to the supermarket.	40	3
• Feeling stressed when things go wrong.	70	7
• Preparing a meal.	30	2

Once this is done and you are satisfied that the steps are not too large, you are ready to carry out the experiments, starting with the easiest situation. Use Worksheet 9.2 to record the belief you are testing, i.e. that you can control your eating, and details of the experiments, as you plan and carry them out.

Worksheet 9.2 Planning and recording behavioural experiments to test thoughts of no control

Thought to be tested:

Belief that the thought is true (0–100%):

Experiment to test thought	Likely problems	Strategies to deal with problems	Date of experiment	Outcome of experiment	Belief in thought (0–100%)

Step 1

Write the thought or thoughts that you are going to test, i.e. that you can control your eating, in your own words, at the top of the worksheet.

Step 2

Rate your belief that the thought is true on a 0 to 100% scale, with 0 being 'I do not believe this thought at all' and 100 being 'I am completely convinced that this thought is true'. Choose the rating that describes your belief in the thought before carrying out the first experiment.

Step 3

Start with the least difficult situation and write what you plan to do in the left hand column under 'experiment to test thought'.

Step 4

To increase your chances of success think about any likely problems, for example, having time on your hands and nothing to occupy you, or feeling upset. Write these under 'likely problems'.

Step 5

Write down how you plan to deal with these problems, if they occur, under 'strategies to deal with problems'.

Step 6

Carry out the first experiment. When you have done this, record the date and brief details of the outcome.

Finally, after completing the experiment and recording the outcome, re-rate belief in the thought that you can control your eating on the same 0–100% scale.

In Box 9.3 you can see Helena's completed worksheet for one of her behavioural experiments. This was an experiment she did after successfully testing out her thought that she could control her eating in several easier situations (taken from her hierarchy of situations in which she was prone to binge).

You should then repeat the whole procedure (from Step 1 to Step 8) for the next most difficult situation, remembering to record your belief in the thought that you can control your eating after completing each experiment. Continue until you reach the top of your list. This will take several days, perhaps several weeks. To help you not to binge, you may also find it useful to draw up an action plan, based around the strategies in Box 9.4.

Box 9.3 Helena's behavioural experiment

Thought to be tested: I can control my eating

Belief that the thought is true (0–100%): 25%

Experiment to test thought	Likely problems	Strategies to deal with problems	Date of experiment	Outcome of experiment	Belief in thought (0–100%)
To control eating at the weekend.	A colleague might offer me food. I might eat it and then go on to binge. I'll be hungry. I'll be tempted to buy chocolate.	Say no. Say I've already eaten. Eat only a small amount. Eat a small meal before going to work on both days. Go to work without any money. Use the 'binge postponement' technique: say 'I won't binge now, I'll wait half an hour'. Stay in public areas.	Saturday and Sunday, 2 and 3 September.	The strategies really helped. Eating before I went to work and keeping it down stopped me from feeling hungry and bingeing at work. Not taking any money out with me stopped me buying chocolate from the shop. I really felt I had control on both days. Feeling that you are losing control is just a feeling, not a fact; you always have a choice.	I can control my eating, 80%.

Box 9.4 The basis of an action plan

- List the advantages and disadvantages of bingeing in this situation.

- Devise a checklist of things that you can do to fill the time left by not bingeing.

- Draw up a list of ways to deal with any discomfort or distress.

- Plan what you can do, practically, to prove to yourself that you do have control.

- Write down (and put into practice) other ways to deal with whatever is concerning you.

Joanna came up with the following advantages and disadvantages of bingeing one afternoon, see Box 9.5. She was feeling upset over a critical remark made to her by a friend about the small amount of lunch she had eaten.

Box 9.5 Joanna's advantages and disadvantages of bingeing

Advantages of bingeing	Disadvantages of bingeing
• It will get it over with and put a stop to my continuous anxiety around food and weight gain. • It will make the criticism hurt less. • It's going to be a bad day from now on – giving in will make me feel better in some way.	• The day will be wasted – I won't manage to accomplish what I set out to do. • It keeps the problem going – it won't stop me worrying about food and about gaining weight in the long term – I worry about these even more after bingeing. • Bingeing makes my mood go up and down so much that people don't know how they will find me. I'm just pushing my friends away, which makes me very unhappy. I'll be in a bad mood for the rest of the afternoon.

Joanna's action plan (based around the strategies in Box 9.6) included ways to distract herself (to fill the time left by not bingeing as well as to deal with any distress) and practical ways to prove to herself that she did have control over her eating. She also drew on the binge postponement strategy that she had previously found helpful.

Box 9.6 Joanna's plan

Distraction

Use distraction (e.g. counting backwards from 100 in 7s; reciting the alphabet backwards, describing an object out loud, practising Spanish). Get absorbed in work – do an easy, but distracting task.

Exposure

Practice control, e.g. buy a small bar of chocolate and eat one square every hour. NB: start with foods that I find easiest to eat, gradually building up to more difficult ones, like crisps and biscuits.

Binge postponement

Use binge postponement strategies.

Negative outcomes

You may be wondering what to do if an experiment doesn't go well. This could happen, particularly at first when you are learning how to plan and carry them out. It may surprise you, but we believe that an unsuccessful outcome is just as useful as a successful outcome. It doesn't mean that you lack self-control. It simply tells you that you need to take a closer look at your plan and carry out a revised experiment, using what you have learned. To do this you will, first of all, need to identify what the problem was. It may help to ask yourself some of the questions in Box 9.7.

Box 9.7 Questions to ask when experiments are unsuccessful

- What did I learn from this?

- Was the situation too difficult?

- Am I expecting too much of myself?

- Did I run out of things to do?

- Did I have enough interesting and enjoyable things planned?

- Did I get very distressed?

- What thoughts did I have?

Debbie was trying to test out her belief that she could control her eating when faced with shopping for clothes. She called a good friend and they arranged to spend the afternoon in town so that Debbie could buy a new pair of trousers. However, as they went into shop after shop nothing seemed to fit or look right. Debbie soon started to think that she was fat and unattractive, particularly when she looked at herself in the changing room mirrors. She didn't manage to buy any trousers and on the way home, to cheer herself up she bought a bar of chocolate. Then, when she got home, she had a binge.

Debbie asked herself the questions in Box 9.7 to try to learn from this. She concluded that, with hindsight, going shopping for trousers had been too difficult. It was too big a step up from her last experiment. She decided that, in future, she must check that what she planned was realistic; and that small steps were important. Most of all, she learned that if a plan went wrong, it was important to learn from it and not punish herself.

Joanna experimented one afternoon with eating one square of chocolate every hour. She ate one square, as planned, for the first three hours. Then she ate the rest of the bar all at once. She immediately thought, 'I just can't control my eating.' After asking herself the questions in Box 9.6 she concluded that she had learned something from what had happened. She found the question 'What thoughts did I have?' particularly useful. It revealed that she had the following unhelpful thoughts: 'I've got to eat it all now, I can't wait until later.' These thoughts had made it easier to eat the rest of the chocolate all at once. She also used what she had learned in Chapter 8 about thinking errors. In particular, she realised that she was focusing simply on one part of what had happened and ignoring the fact that she had succeeded with the task for the first three hours.

Summary exercise

Write a brief summary of what you have learned from this chapter; both from the information presented and from the exercises. Also write down how you will put what you have learned into practice. Then, write the essence of your summary and plans on a small index card. Put this in a bag or inside a diary that you usually carry with you and make time, twice a day, to read the card.

Chapter summary

This chapter has focused on helping you to confirm and build up a sense that you have control over your eating. The following important points were made:

- Graded behavioural experiments can be used to confirm and build up your sense of control.

- In a behavioural experiment a negative outcome is just as useful as a positive outcome.

We made the following suggestion to help you identify the evidence you are using to support the belief that you can't control your eating and, most importantly, to build up your sense of control:

- Carry out a series of graded behavioural experiments to confirm and build up your sense of control.

CHAPTER 10

Identifying Permissive Thoughts

You have already worked on identifying and challenging one type of thought: the thought that you can't control your eating. Now it is time to learn how to identify (and, in the next chapter, how to challenge) permissive thoughts. These beliefs are particularly important in keeping bingeing going once it has started. They give you permission. They allow you to feel it's OK to eat more and more, and then to binge. They are also known as the 'what the hell' effect. Caroline ate rather more than she had planned. She thought, 'What the hell, I've blown my diet. I might as well keep eating.'

Permissive thoughts

Permissive thoughts are closely related to thoughts of no control and, like these, they keep eating going once it has started. Examples of permissive thoughts can be seen in Box 10.1.

Box 10.1 Permissive thoughts, some examples

- I might just as well carry on eating now I've started.
- I'm going to get rid of it later.
- This is the last time I can have all I want.
- This is my reward for not eating earlier today.
- I have to eat right now.
- I'll start again tomorrow.
- Another bite won't hurt.
- I'll just make it a small binge.
- I'll just have one more biscuit…

Identifying permissive thoughts at the time they occur

It is important that you learn to identify permissive thoughts at the time they occur. This will enable you to catch and, later, to challenge them early on; well before you resort to bingeing. Identifying these thoughts takes a bit of practice. We have devised two ways to help you. First, a brief questionnaire will help you to discover the extent to which these thoughts typically occur in your bingeing vicious circles. Second, and perhaps most importantly, we will take you through a worksheet that will help you identify examples of these types of thoughts, in your own words, when they occur in practice.

Questionnaire to identify permissive thoughts

Completing the permissive thoughts questionnaire (Questionnaire 10.1) will help you to find out how far permissive thoughts may be involved in maintaining your bingeing vicious circles. Read the instructions carefully before you complete it.

Meaning of scores

To find out your score, add up the ratings given to each thought. Then divide the total by the number of questions, i.e. 7. This will give you an idea of how much you believe, in general, in your permissive thoughts. To interpret your score look in Box 10.2.

Box 10.2 Meaning of questionnaire scores

0–9	Low score. Little or no belief; unlikely to be too much of a problem for you.
10–29	Moderate score. Moderate belief; likely to be somewhat of a problem for you.
30–59	High score. High belief; likely to be quite a big problem for you.
60–100	Very high score. Very high belief; likely to be a major problem for you.

In addition to the thoughts on the questionnaire you will probably have other examples of permissive thoughts. We will help you to identify these, and the time at which they occur using the thoughts record.

Identifying permissive thoughts in everyday life: The thoughts record

The questionnaire will have given you an idea of the extent to which permissive thoughts may be a problem for you. However, as we noted above, it is particularly important to identify thoughts in your own words, and at the time they occur. We suggest that from now on you start to keep a detailed record of these thoughts in situations in which you have binged. Worksheet 10.1 will help you with this. As you can see there are three columns: 'situation (including activating events)', 'feelings' and 'permissive thoughts'. The record is an expanded example of an A-B-C analysis. Activating events or As are the events that activate or trigger distress. Permissive thoughts are the bad thoughts or Bs that result. Feelings are the Cs or consequences of the thoughts. Eating or bingeing is also a C, or possible consequence of having such thoughts. As before, thoughts play a key role. By learning how to challenge these (see the next chapter) you will learn how to reduce distressing feelings and to break the cycle of thoughts, feelings and behaviours that maintains bingeing.

Questionnaire 10.1 Permissive thoughts questionnaire

Instructions

Listed below are some thoughts which people sometimes have just before eating turns into a binge. Please read each thought carefully and decide how much you believe each thought to be true. Choose the rating which best describes how you usually feel just before your eating becomes a binge rather than how you feel right now. Write the number in the space before the thought.

Rating Scale

0   10   20   30   40   50   60   70   80   90   100

I do not
usually
believe this
at all

I am usually
completely
convinced
that this is
true

Questions

1. ...... Now I've started eating I might as well carry on.

2. ...... One more bite won't hurt.

3. ...... I've nothing apart from bingeing in my life.

4. ...... I'm fat anyway, it doesn't matter if I get fatter.

5. ...... I don't seem to be losing weight, more food won't hurt.

6. ...... I deserve something nice.

7. ...... Go on, eat more to punish yourself.

Using a thoughts record to record permissive thoughts

To help you identify your permissive thoughts, the thoughts record asks you to respond to a series of questions; Worksheet 10.1 has the questions written on it. Answering the questions immediately after bingeing will help you to identify permissive thoughts.

Worksheet 10.1 Identifying permissive thoughts using a thoughts record		
Situation	**Feelings and sensations**	**Permissive thoughts**
• When was it? • Where were you? • Who were you with? • What were you doing? • What were you thinking about?	• What feelings did you have? • What body sensations did you notice?	• What were you saying to yourself that made it easier to keep eating? • Identify and circle the hot thought. This is the thought that makes it most likely that you will binge.

A completed example

An example of a form completed by Emma can be seen in Box 10.3

Box 10.3 Emma's completed worksheet: Identifying permissive thoughts

Situation	Feelings and sensations	Permissive thoughts
Friday, at college, alone, had a free period, thinking about my assignment (how difficult it was going to be). Ate a bar of chocolate, knew I was going to binge. Got on the bus to town, went to Burger King – had a burger, two portions of fries, a milkshake, one big bar of chocolate, another smaller bar of chocolate	Anxious Heavy Blank	I might as well keep eating now I've started. I can make myself sick afterwards – so it doesn't matter – I can have what I want and I won't gain weight. I might as well carry on until my money has run out. I've got to eat more and more.
• When was it? • Where were you? • Who were you with? • What were you doing? • What were you thinking about?	• What feelings did you have? • What body sensations did you notice?	• What were you saying to yourself that made it easier to keep eating? • Identify and circle the hot thought. This is the thought that makes it most likely that you will binge.

Using the form for yourself

Because it is important to capture thoughts at the time they occur, make sure that you have a copy of the thoughts record with you at all times. Get it out and complete it immediately after each binge in the next week or two. To help you, we will talk you through the form; follow the step by step instructions below each time you complete it.

STEP 1

Notice and record the activating event for your bingeing. When was it? Where were you? Who were you with? What were you doing? What were you thinking? Make a note of this under 'situation' in column 1.

STEP 2

What feelings (e.g. sadness, tension, anxiety) did you notice just before you binged? What body sensations did you notice just before you binged? Make a note of these under 'feelings and sensations' in column 2.

STEP 3

What were the thoughts that you had immediately before eating turned into a binge. Write the thoughts in column 3, under 'permissive thoughts'.

STEP 4

Which thought was the hot thought? The hot thought is the thought that makes it most likely that you will go on to eat more and more and to binge. Circle the hot thought in column 3.

This exercise may seem time consuming but you are learning how to build up a detailed picture of what keeps your bingeing going. It is important to do this so that you can, in the next chapter, learn how to challenge your thoughts. Practice completing a thoughts record for your permissive thoughts whenever possible over the next week or two. The more you practise, the easier it will be to identify them.

Summary exercise

Write a brief summary of what you have learned from this chapter; both from the information presented and from the exercises. Also write down how you will put what you have learned into practice. Then, write the essence of your summary and plans on a small index card. Put this in a bag or inside a diary that you usually carry with you and make time, twice a day, to read the card.

Chapter summary

This chapter has helped you identify examples of the permissive thoughts that keep your bingeing going in your everyday life. The following points were made:

- It is important to identify permissive thoughts at the time they occur.
- The thoughts record is an expanded version of an A-B-C analysis. Feelings and eating (or bingeing) are the consequences or Cs of the permissive thoughts or Bs.
- Identifying thoughts takes a bit of practice.
- Catching thoughts early on will enable you, in later chapters, to challenge them before you eat more and more and end up having a binge.
- The questionnaire in this chapter can be used to help you identify your permissive thoughts.

- Most importantly, a thoughts record will help you identify these thoughts in your everyday life

The following suggestions were made:

- Use the thoughts questionnaire to identify your permissive thoughts.

- Assess the meaning of your score.

- Use the thoughts record to identify your permissive thoughts in everyday life.

- Carry a copy of the thoughts record at all times and complete one immediately after each episode of bingeing for the next week or two.

CHAPTER 11

Challenging Permissive Thoughts

In Chapter 9 you used behavioural experiments to challenge your thoughts of no control. In this chapter we will introduce you to a way of challenging your thoughts using a written record sheet: an expanded version of the thoughts record (introduced in the last chapter). The aim is the same as it was with thoughts of no control: to arrive at an alternative, more balanced and more realistic conclusion. The thoughts that we will show you how to challenge are the permissive thoughts which you began to record in the last chapter.

Challenging permissive thoughts using a written record

In Chapter 10 we introduced you to the idea of a hot thought. This is the thought which makes it most likely that you will carry on eating once you have started and go on to binge. It is particularly important that you learn to challenge these hot thoughts. They are very important in maintaining bingeing.

Useful questions to help you challenge permissive thoughts

Challenging thoughts effectively takes practice; the more you practise the better you will get at generating alternatives. To help you we have devised some useful questions. Some are general questions, and will be useful for challenging all types of thought, including any of your remaining thoughts of no control (and the positive beliefs about eating covered in the next two chapters). We have also devised some specific questions, designed especially to help you with permissive thoughts. The general questions can be seen in Box 11.1. The more specific questions can be seen in Box 11.2.

Exercise: Using the thoughts record to challenge permissive thoughts

Your thoughts record, on which you have been identifying permissive thoughts can be expanded to include some additional columns (see Worksheet 11.1). The additional columns are to be used for challenging the permissive thoughts that you have been recording.

Box 11.1 Useful general questions to help you challenge permissive thoughts

---

General questions

The counter-evidence

What counter-evidence do I have?

Do I have any evidence that shows that this thought is not 100% true all the time?

What would I say to someone else?

What you would say to someone else

If my best friend or someone close to me had this thought, what would I tell them?

Asking your best friend

What would someone else say about this thought?

If my best friend or someone close to me knew I was thinking this thought, what would they say to me?

What evidence would they use that would suggest that my thought was not 100% true all the time?

Looking at your experience

What have I learned from the past?

What have I learned from bingeing and vomiting in the past that could help me now? When I have had this thought before, what helped me not to binge and vomit?

Is this situation similar to past situations?

Thinking errors

What errors in thinking am I making?

Am I jumping to conclusions that are not completely justified by the evidence?

Am I forgetting, discounting or minimising relevant facts?

Am I thinking in all-or-nothing terms? In reality, is it more likely that there are shades of grey?

Am I being misled by how I feel inside, instead of focusing on the facts?

Box 11.2 Useful specific questions to help you challenge permissive thoughts

Specific questions

What are the consequences of thinking like this?

Do these thoughts make it easier or harder to binge?

Is it really true, in the end, that bingeing doesn't matter?

What could I say to myself that would make it more difficult to binge?

Is it really true that I've nothing else in my life?

If there really is very little, how can I change that?

How could I be nice to myself, apart from bingeing?

Worksheet 11.1 Thoughts record for challenging permissive thoughts about eating

Situation	Feelings and sensations	Permissive thoughts	Evidence that does not support the hot thought	Alternative, more helpful thought	Belief in alternative thought
• When was it? • Where were you? • Who were you with? • What were you doing? • What were you thinking about?	• How were you feeling? • What body sensations did you notice?	• What were you saying that made it easier to keep eating? • Identify and circle the hot thought. This is the thought that makes it most likely that you will keep eating and go on to binge.	• Use the questions in Boxes 11.1 and 11.2 to challenge your hot thought.	• Write down an alternative, more helpful thought.	• Rate how much you believe this thought to be true on a scale from 0 to 100%.

In this section we will talk you step by step through the process of challenging one of your 'hot' permissive thoughts.

Step 1

Record a situation in which you binged and vomited, just as you did in the last chapter, but this time using the expanded thoughts record. Fill in the first three columns as before, noting your permissive thoughts.

Step 2

Identify the hot thought, as before. Look for this in column 3. Put a circle around it.

Step 3

In the column 'Evidence that does not support the hot thought', list all the evidence that suggests that the thought is not true. This should be recorded in column 4.

Step 4

Use the general and specific questions in Boxes 11.1 and 11.2 to help you come up with an alternative, more balanced and more realistic thought. Record this thought in column 5, the column labelled 'alternative, more realistic thought'.

Step 5

Rate how much you believe the alternative thought to be true on a scale from 0 to 100%, with 0 being 'I do not believe this thought at all' and 100 being 'I am completely convinced that this thought is true'.

Not all the questions in Box 11.1 and Box 11.2 will be useful each time; choose those that seem most appropriate.

In Box 11.3 below you can see Gerrie's completed record. She used the general and specific questions in Boxes 11.1 and 11.2 to help her challenge her permissive thoughts. She found it particularly useful to examine the evidence for and against her 'hot' thought, and to consider what she would say to someone else in the same predicament. She also asked herself, 'what would my best friend say about this?', looked at what she had learned from her own experience and, finally, identified the thinking errors she was making.

She also found it helpful to write down the questions that she found most useful on a small index card. She carried this around with her, read it two or three times a day and, if she felt tempted to binge, got it out and responded to the questions. She found this extremely useful in interrupting the vicious circle that led to a binge.

You will need to practise challenging your thoughts as often as you can. Keep an expanded thoughts record with you at all times and, if you have a binge, record and challenge your permissive thoughts as soon as possible after it has occurred. If you complete this exercise regularly then you should find that, with practice, belief in the problematic thoughts decreases. As this happens, the desire to keep eating more and more will fall, so that gradually you will be able to stop bingeing.

Box 11.3 Gerrie's completed worksheet: Challenging permissive thoughts

Situation	Feelings and sensations	Permissive thoughts	Evidence that does not support the hot thought	Alternative, more helpful thought	Belief in alternative thought
Monday evening, in the kitchen, alone, planning what to have for supper, thinking about the pressures of the day and not being able to escape from them. Ate a biscuit with my coffee.	Anxious Panicky Shaky Uncomfortable feeling in my stomach.	I might just as well carry on now. I've got to eat more than this. I'll make myself sick afterwards.	Although I feel anxious/ uncomfortable now, bingeing and vomiting will make me feel far worse than this.	Just because I feel anxious/uncomfortable doesn't mean that the best thing to do is to carry on eating. I'll only feel worse if I go on. **What you would say to someone else?** Eating more/bingeing will only make me feel even more of a failure. **Asking your best friend?** My best friend, Leonie, would point out all the nice things about me and ask me to stop. **Looking at your experience** Thinking like this just makes it easier to binge. **Thinking errors** This is all or nothing thinking – just because I've eaten one biscuit doesn't mean I have to have a huge binge.	65%
• When was it? • Where were you? • Who were you with? • What were you doing? • What were you thinking about?	• How were you feeling? • What body sensations did you notice?	• What were you saying that made it easier to keep eating? • Identify and circle the hot thought. This is the thought that makes it most likely that you will keep eating and go on to binge.	• Use the questions in Boxes 11.1 and 11.2 to challenge your hot thought.	• Write down an alternative, more helpful thought.	• Rate how much you believe this thought to be true on a scale from 0 to 100%

When progress is slow

If you find that your belief in the hot thoughts is not declining as quickly as you would like, and it is difficult to generate and believe in alternative thoughts, don't despair. One possibility is that you are expecting too much of yourself too quickly. The other possibility is that you have some 'yes, but' thoughts, like those we warned you about in Chapter 8.

'Yes, but' thoughts

You can deal with these thoughts in the way we suggested in Chapter 8. Work with the alternative thought you have generated, and that you would like to believe more. Identify precisely what the 'yes, but' thought linked to it is. You can then use the general and specific questions in Box 11.1 and Box 11.2, as appropriate, to challenge it. You may need to repeat the process of asking whether there are any 'yes but' thoughts and challenging those in turn, until your belief in the initial thought has fallen to a relatively low level. Ultimately your goal should be to reduce belief in all the problematic thoughts to zero. Look in Box 11.4 at Diane's example of a series of 'yes, but' thoughts and how she challenged them to help you.

Box 11.4 Diane's 'yes, but' chain of thoughts

Permissive thought	Alternative, more helpful response
• I haven't got the strength to stop.	• Even though I feel tired and miserable, I do have a choice – I can choose to stop.
• Yes, but it doesn't feel like it.	• That's emotional reasoning – just because I feel I don't have a choice doesn't mean I don't.
• Yes, but because I feel so tired and miserable, surely I deserve a treat.	• It won't feel like a treat afterwards – there are other ways to be nice to myself – what would I say to a friend?

Summary exercise

Write a brief summary of what you have learned from this chapter; both from the information presented and from the exercises. Also write down how you will put what you have learned into practice. Then, write the essence of your summary and plans on a small index card. Put this in a bag or inside a diary that you usually carry with you and make time, twice a day, to read the card.

Chapter summary

This chapter has introduced ways to challenge permissive thoughts using a written record: the thoughts record. It made the following important points:

- The aim is the same as it was for behavioural experiments: to arrive at an alternative, more balanced and more realistic conclusion.

- The most important principle is to make sure you examine all the evidence.

- It is also important to ask: What would I say to someone else? What would my best friend say? What have I learned from my experience? What thinking error could I be making?

- Challenging thoughts effectively takes practice.

- Ultimately, belief in the thoughts should decline to zero.

The following suggestions were made:

- Use the thoughts record, and the general and specific questions we have devised to challenge your hot permissive thoughts.

- Carry a thoughts record at all times and use it to identify and challenge permissive thoughts as soon as possible after every binge.

- If progress is slow make sure that you are not expecting too much too soon. Check and challenge any 'yes, but' thoughts.

CHAPTER 12

Identifying Positive Beliefs about Eating

Now that you have learned how to identify and challenge permissive thoughts, it is time to move on to positive beliefs about eating. These beliefs are particularly important in starting off the eating that will turn into a binge.

This chapter will teach you how to identify these beliefs in practice. The next chapter will teach you how to challenge them.

Box 12.1 Positive beliefs about eating: Some examples

How eating will help:

- Eating takes my mind off worries.

- Eating stops me feeling so bad about myself.

- Eating will help me get back in touch with myself.

- Bulimia nervosa (bingeing) is my best friend; it never lets me down.

- Eating makes me feel safe.

- When I eat, it's the only time I'm happy.

- Food is a great comforter.

What will happen if you don't eat:

- If I don't eat then I won't be able to cope.

- If I don't eat I'll have to face up to all my problems; that will be intolerable.

- If I don't eat I'll feel worse and worse; I won't be able to stand it.

Positive beliefs about eating

There are two sides to positive eating beliefs. First, there are beliefs about how eating will be helpful (particularly in dealing with any negative thoughts and feelings that you may have about yourself). Second (the flip side), there may be beliefs about what will happen if you don't start eating. Both are important. Look in Box 12.1 to see examples of some of the positive beliefs about eating that our patients have had.

Identifying positive beliefs about eating at the time they occur

As with permissive thoughts, it is important that you learn to identify positive beliefs about eating at the time they occur. This will enable you to catch and later to challenge them early on; well before you resort to bingeing. As you will know by now, identifying thoughts takes a bit of practice. As for permissive thoughts, we have devised two ways to help you identify your positive beliefs about eating.

First, there is a brief questionnaire to complete. Second, and perhaps most importantly, we will take you through a worksheet (similar to the thoughts record used in Chapter 10 to identify permissive thoughts) that will help you identify examples of these types of thoughts, in your own words, at the time they occur.

Questionnaire to identify positive beliefs about eating

Completing the positive beliefs about eating questionnaire (Questionnaire 12.1) will help you to find out how far positive beliefs about eating are involved in maintaining your bingeing. Read the instructions carefully before you complete it.

Meaning of scores

To find out your score, add up the ratings given to each thought. Then divide the total by the number of questions, i.e. 10. This will give you an idea of how much you believe, in general, in your positive beliefs about eating. To interpret your score look in Box 12.2.

Box 12.2 Meaning of questionnaire scores

0–9	Low score. Little or no belief; unlikely to be too much of a problem for you.
10–29	Moderate score. Moderate belief; likely to be somewhat of a problem for you.
30–59	High score. High belief; likely to be a big problem for you.
60–100	Very high score. Very high belief; likely to be a major problem for you.

Questionnaire 12.1 Positive beliefs about eating questionnaire

Instructions

Listed below are some thoughts which people sometimes have when just starting to eat/binge. Please read each thought carefully and decide how much you believe each thought to be true. Choose the rating which best describes how you usually feel just before bingeing rather than how you feel right now. Write the number in the space before the thought.

Rating Scale

0 10 20 30 40 50 60 70 80 90 100

I do not
usually
believe
this at all

I am usually
completely
convinced
that this is
true

Questions

1. ...... Eating will take away/distract me from the bad feelings.

2. ...... Eating means I don't have to think about unpleasant things.

3. ...... If I eat it will all hurt less inside.

4. ...... Eating will fill the emptiness inside me.

5. ...... Eating will stop me feeling bored.

6. ...... Eating will comfort me, it's a way of being nice to myself.

7. ...... If I don't eat then the bad feelings will get worse and worse.

8. ...... If I don't eat I'll lose control.

9. ...... I can't do anything when I feel bad except eat.

10. ...... My life feels empty if I'm not bingeing and vomiting.

The meaning of not bingeing

We have already noted that there are two types of positive beliefs about eating. First, there are the beliefs that eating will help with negative thoughts and negative feelings. Second, there are beliefs about the negative consequences of not eating. These are represented by questions 7, 8 and 10. To see how much of a problem these thoughts are for you, add up your scores to each of these three questions and divide by the number of questions, i.e. 3. To interpret your scores use Box 12.1 above.

Identifying positive beliefs about eating in everyday life: the thoughts record

The positive beliefs about eating questionnaire will have given you an idea of how much you believe your positive beliefs about eating. However, as we noted in Chapter 10, it is particularly important to identify thoughts at the time they occur. We suggest that from now on you start to keep a detailed record of your positive beliefs about eating. Worksheet 12.1 will help you identify and provide a record of these thoughts. The record is very similar to the thoughts record (Worksheet 10.1) in Chapter 10, which you used to identify your permissive thoughts. There are three columns, 'situation (including activating event)', 'feelings' and 'positive beliefs about eating'. As we noted in Chapter 10, this is an expanded example of an A-B-C analysis. Activating events or As are the triggers of distress, Bs or positive thoughts about eating are the thoughts that result. Cs or consequences are the feelings and behaviour (in this case the behaviour is eating which leads to bingeing) that result from the thoughts.

Using a thoughts record to record positive beliefs about eating

To help you identify your positive beliefs about eating, the thoughts record asks you to respond to a series of questions. Worksheet 12.1 has the questions written on it. Answering the questions immediately after bingeing will help you to identify your positive beliefs related to eating.

A completed example

An example of a form completed by Maria can be seen in Box 12.3.

Box 12.3 Maria's completed worksheet: Identifying positive beliefs about eating

Situation	Feelings and sensations	Positive thoughts about eating
Yesterday evening, at home, alone, trying to watch TV, thinking about an argument with Richard earlier in the day, thinking about food.	Sad Depressed	Eating will distract me from thoughts of food. Eating means I won't have to think how horrible, selfish and thoughtless I am.
• When was it? • Where were you? • Who were you with? • What were you doing? • What were you thinking about?	• How did you feel? • What body sensations did you notice?	• How did you think eating would help? • What were you afraid might happen if you didn't eat? • Identify and circle the hot thought. This is the thought that makes it most likely that you will eat/binge.

Worksheet 12.1 Identifying positive beliefs about eating using a thoughts record

Situation	Feelings and sensations	Positive beliefs about eating
• When was it? • Where were you? • Who were you with? • What were you doing? • What were you thinking about?	• How did you feel? • What body sensations did you notice?	• How did you think eating would help? • What were you afraid might happen if you didn't eat? • Identify and circle the hot thought. This is the thought that makes it most likely that you will eat/binge.

Using the form for yourself

Because it is important to capture thoughts at the time they occur, make sure, as before, that you have a copy of this thoughts record (Worksheet 12.1) with you at all times. Get it out and complete it immediately after each binge in the next week or two. To help you, we will talk you through the form. Follow the step-by-step instructions below each time you complete it.

Step 1

Notice and record the activating event or trigger for your bingeing. When was it? Where were you? Who were you with? What were you doing? Make a note of this under 'situation' in column 1.

Step 2

What feelings and body sensations did you notice just before you started to eat? Make a note of these under 'feelings and sensations' in column 2.

Step 3

What were the thoughts that you had just before bingeing? In particular, how did you think eating would help? What did you think would happen if you didn't eat? Write the thoughts under 'positive beliefs about eating' in column 4.

Step 4

Which thought was the hot thought? Which thought made it most likely that you would start eating? Circle the hot thought in column 4.

Like the parallel exercise in Chapter 10, this exercise may also seem time consuming but you are continuing to build up a detailed picture of what keeps your bingeing going. It is important to do this so that you can, in the next chapter, learn how to challenge your positive beliefs about eating. Practise completing a thoughts record whenever possible over the next week or two; the more you practise the easier it will be to identify the thoughts.

Summary exercise

Write a brief summary of what you have learned from this chapter; both from the information presented and from the exercises. Also write down how you will put what you have learned into practice. Then, write the essence of your summary and plans on a small index card. Put this in a bag or inside a diary that you carry with you most of the time and make time, twice a day, to read the card.

Chapter summary

This chapter has helped you start to identify examples of the positive beliefs about eating that are involved in keeping your bingeing going in your everyday life. The following important points were made:

- It is important to identify positive beliefs about eating at the time they occur.

- The thoughts record is an expanded version of an A-B-C analysis. Feelings and eating are the consequences or Cs of the positive beliefs about eating or Bs.

- Identifying thoughts takes a bit of practice.

- Catching thoughts early on will enable you, in later chapters, to challenge them before you resort to bingeing.

- A questionnaire can be used to help you identify your positive beliefs about eating.

- Most importantly, a thoughts record will help you identify thoughts in your everyday life.

The following suggestions were made:

- Use the positive beliefs about eating questionnaire to identify your positive beliefs about eating.

- Assess the meaning of your score.

- Use the thoughts record to identify your positive beliefs about eating in your everyday life.

- Carry a copy of the thoughts record at all times and complete one immediately after each episode of bingeing for the next week or two.

CHAPTER 13

Challenging Positive Beliefs about Eating

In this chapter we will introduce you to a way of challenging your positive beliefs about eating using a written record; an expanded version of the thoughts record (introduced in the last chapter). The aim is the same as it was in Chapter 11 where you learned how to challenge permissive thoughts: to arrive at an alternative, more balanced and more realistic conclusion.

Challenging thoughts using a written record

We have already discussed the idea of a hot thought. In Chapter 10 the hot permissive thought was the thought that made it most likely that you would eat more and more and go on to binge. Here the hot positive thought about eating is the one that makes it most likely that you will start eating. As before, we suggest you focus on challenging your hot thoughts.

Important principles

THE COUNTER-EVIDENCE

As before, perhaps the most important principle in learning how to challenge thoughts using a written record is to make sure you examine all the evidence against your thought. Make sure you ask yourself what evidence you have against it, and whether you have any evidence which suggests that it is not completely true all the time.

WHAT YOU WOULD SAY TO SOMEONE ELSE

It is often useful to ask what you would say to someone else who had the thought that you are trying to challenge. This may reveal that you have different (usually higher) standards and expectations for yourself than you would have for other people.

ASKING YOUR BEST FRIEND

It can be useful to ask not only what evidence you have yourself that a thought is not true but what you think someone else, ideally a close friend, would say to you about it. This question may reveal that you have different (again, usually higher) standards and expectations of yourself than others have of you.

LOOKING AT YOUR EXPERIENCE

Looking at what you have learned about your eating disorder from past experience can be useful, particularly asking yourself what has helped you with the thought when you have had it before.

Thinking errors

Like permissive thoughts, positive beliefs about eating may reflect certain errors in thinking. You may be able to find several types of thinking error, including: selective attention; jumping to unjustified conclusions; forgetting, discounting or minimising relevant facts; thinking in all or nothing terms; and being misled by feelings instead of focusing on the facts.

Behavioural experiments

Your thought may be a fear, or a prediction, about what might happen (for example, about what might happen if you don't go ahead and eat/binge). If this is the case then, as well as challenging the thought using a written record, it may be useful to devise a behavioural experiment to test it. This will enable you to see whether what you fear, in the worst case scenario, really does occur.

Useful questions to help you challenge positive beliefs about eating

As we noted in Chapter 11, challenging thoughts effectively takes practice; the more you practise the better you will get at generating alternatives. To help you challenge your positive beliefs about eating we have devised some useful questions. Some are general questions, covering the points raised above, and will be useful for challenging all types of thought, including any of your remaining thoughts of no control and the permissive thoughts covered in Chapter 11. They are similar (but not identical) to the general questions in Chapter 11. We repeat them here for ease of reference.

We have also devised some specific questions, designed especially to help you with positive beliefs about eating. The general questions can be seen in Box 13.1. The more specific questions can be seen in Box 13.2.

Box 13.1 Useful general questions to help you challenge positive beliefs about eating

General questions

The counter-evidence

- What counter-evidence do I have?

- Do I have any evidence that shows that this thought is not 100% true all the time?

What you would say to someone else

- What would I say to someone else?

- If my best friend or someone close to me had this thought, what would I tell them?

Asking your best friend

- What would someone else say about this thought?

- If my best friend or someone close to me knew I was thinking this thought, what would they say to me?

- What evidence would they use that would suggest that my thought was not 100% true all the time?

Looking at your experience

- What have I learned from the past?

- What have I learned from bingeing and vomiting in the past that could help me now? When I have had this thought before, what did I think that helped me not to eat/binge and vomit?

- Is this situation similar to past situations?

Thinking errors

- What errors in thinking am I making?

- Am I jumping to conclusions that are not completely justified by the evidence?

- Am I forgetting, discounting or minimising relevant facts?

- Am I thinking in all-or-nothing terms? In reality, is it more likely that there are shades of grey?

- Am I being misled by how I feel inside, instead of focusing on the facts?

Box 13.2 Useful specific questions to help you challenge positive beliefs about eating

Specific questions

Thoughts that eating will be helpful

- Is this a short-sighted view?

- How will I feel later, if I go ahead?

- What have I learned from the bingeing vicious circle?

Thoughts about the consequences of not eating

- What's the very worst that might happen if I don't binge?

- Realistically, what is most likely to happen?

- Would that be so terrible?

- Would it be worse then bingeing?

- How can I test my prediction?

- If I do feel distressed, how can I deal with the distress without eating?

- What can I do instead of eating?

Using the thoughts record to challenge positive beliefs about eating

Your thoughts record, on which you have been identifying positive beliefs about eating, can be expanded to include some additional columns (Worksheet 13.1). The additional columns are to be used for challenging the positive beliefs about eating that you began to record in the last chapter.

In this section we will talk you step by step through the process of challenging one of your 'hot' positive beliefs about eating.

Worksheet 13.1 Thoughts record for challenging positive beliefs about eating

Situation	Feelings and sensations	Positive thoughts about eating	Evidence that does not support the hot thought	Alternative, more helpful thought	Belief in alternative thought
• When was it? • Where were you? • Who were you with? • What were you doing? • What were you thinking about?	• How did you feel? • What body sensations did you notice?	• What were you saying that made it easier to start eating? • Identify and circle the hot thought. This is the thought that makes it most likely that you will start eating and go on to binge	• Use the questions in Boxes 13.1 and 13.2 to challenge your hot thought	• Write down an alternative, more helpful thought	• Rate how much you believe this thought to be true on a scale from 0 to 100%

Step 1

Record a situation in which you binged and vomited, just as you did in Chapter 12, but this time using the expanded thoughts record. Fill in the first three columns as before, noting your positive beliefs about eating.

Step 2

Identify the hot thought, as before. Look for this in column 3.

Step 3

In the column 'evidence that does not support the hot thought', list all the evidence that suggests that the thought is not true. This should be recorded in column 4.

Step 4

Use the general and specific questions in Boxes 13.1 and 13.2 to help you come up with an alternative, more balanced and more realistic thought. Record this thought in column 5, labelled 'alternative, more realistic thought'. Not all the questions in Boxes 13.1 and 13.2 will be useful each time; choose those that seem most appropriate.

Step 5

Rate how much you believe the alternative thought to be true on a scale from 0 to 100%.

Take a look at Margaret's completed record in Box 13.3 to help you. One of her positive beliefs about eating was 'eating will make me feel better'. The flip side of that was the thought 'if I don't eat I won't be able to cope with the distress of feeling so bad/worried'. Both thoughts were equally important to her. This meant that both were hot thoughts and needed to be challenged. (This can happen with positive thoughts about eating, the initial thought and the flip side of it may be equally important, and both may need to be challenged.) Margaret looked at the evidence for and against the thought and its flip side. She also looked at what she would say to someone else who had these thoughts, at what her best friend would say, at what her experience of having an eating problem had taught her and, finally, at any thinking errors she was making.

Box 13.3 Margaret's completed worksheet: challenging positive beliefs about eating

Situation	Feelings and sensations	Positive thoughts about eating	Evidence that does not support the hot thought	Alternative, more helpful thought	Belief in alternative thought
This morning, at home, alone, trying to finish a letter, thinking about the party last night. Thinking that I'd had fun, felt wanted and been popular. Had the thought 'I had a lovely time, now it will all go wrong.' • When was it? • Where were you? • Who were you with? • What were you doing? • What were you thinking about?	Low in mood Anxious Twitchy • How did you feel? • What body sensations did you notice?	Eating will make me feel better. If I don't eat I won't be able to cope with the distress of feeling so worried/bad • What were you saying that made it easier to start eating? Identify and circle the hot thought. This is the thought that makes it most likely that you will start eating and go on to binge.	Feeling better doesn't last. After stopping eating all the original thoughts are still there, plus then I'm worried about getting fat – that ruins my day. When I've felt upset and not binged, it's never been as bad as I've feared (e.g. when my boyfriend finished with me I felt like bingeing but went out with my flatmate instead – by the end of the evening I no longer wanted to binge). **What would you say to someone else?** Don't do it. It's not worth it. Bingeing will make you feel even more depressed and the problem is still there. **Asking your best friend** Sarah would point out all the negatives about bingeing. She's noticed I'm subdued and distant when I've been bingeing and that I generally look very unhappy. **Looking at your experience** It helps to distract myself, keep busy. Plan to be in situations where bingeing is difficult, e.g. with friends. Put the problem in perspective. Talk to my mum or Ellie, they always have good advice. **Thinking errors** Jumping to conclusions – assuming when I feel bad that bingeing is the only solution to feeling better. • Use the questions in Boxes 13.1 and 13.2 to challenge your hot thought.	Eating/bingeing never makes me feel better. There are other ways to cope with feeling upset. • Write down an alternative, more helpful thought	65% • Rate how much you believe this thought to be true on a scale from 0 to 100%

You will need to practise challenging your thoughts as often as you can. Continue to keep an expanded thoughts record with you at all times and, if you have a binge, record and challenge your positive beliefs about eating as soon as possible after it has occurred.

If you complete this exercise regularly then you should find that, with practice, belief in the problematic thoughts decreases. As this happens, your desire and urge to binge will fall, and you will gradually be able to stop doing it. This written strategy is particularly powerful and effective if you can use it together with the strategies learned in Chapter 9 to delay bingeing. Postponing or delaying bingeing will give you a chance to try out the new strategies you have learned in this chapter. Using these two strategies together will decrease your urge to binge, and actual binges, more quickly.

When progress is slow

If you find that your belief in the thoughts is not declining as quickly as you would like, don't despair. One possibility is that you are expecting too much of yourself too quickly. The other possibility is that you have some 'yes, but' thoughts, like those we warned you about in Chapter 8.

'Yes, but' thoughts

You can deal with these thoughts in the way we suggested in Chapter 8. Work with the alternative thought you have generated, which you would like to believe more. Identify precisely what the 'yes, but' thought linked to it. You can then use the general and specific questions in Boxes 13.1 and 13.2, as appropriate, to challenge it. You may need to repeat the process of asking whether there are any 'yes, but' thoughts and challenging those in turn, until your belief in the initial thought has fallen to a relatively low level. As for thoughts of no control and permissive thoughts, your goal should be to reduce belief in all the problematic thoughts to zero.

Summary exercise

Write a brief summary of what you have learned from this chapter; both from the information presented and from the exercises. Also write down how you will put what you have learned into practice. Then, write the essence of your summary and plans on a small index card. Put this in a bag or inside a diary that you carry with you most of the time and make time, twice a day, to read the card.

Chapter summary

This chapter has introduced ways to challenge positive beliefs about eating using a written record, the thoughts record. It made the following important points:

- The aim is the same as it was for behavioural experiments; to arrive at an alternative, more balanced and more realistic conclusion.
- The most important principle is to make sure you examine all the evidence.
- It is also important to ask: What would I say to someone else? What would my best friend say? What have I learned from my experience? What thinking error could I be making?
- Challenging thoughts effectively takes practice.
- Ultimately, belief in the thoughts should decline to zero.

The following suggestions were made:

- Use the thoughts record and the general and specific questions we have devised, to challenge your hot positive beliefs about eating.
- If progress is slow, make sure that you are not expecting too much too soon. Check and challenge any 'yes, but' thoughts.
- Carry a thoughts record at all times and use it to identify and challenge positive beliefs about eating as soon as possible after every binge.
- The strategy is particularly powerful if used together with strategies learned to delay bingeing in Chapter 10.

CHAPTER 14

Changing Behaviours

In the last few chapters you have identified and challenged some of the thoughts that keep your bingeing going. In this chapter we will explore how certain types of behaviours can keep bad or negative thoughts about your weight and shape alive. In this chapter we will discuss how engaging in certain behaviours can maintain negative thoughts about your weight and shape. We will help you to identify what behaviours maintain your own negative thoughts and, towards the end of the chapter, suggest ways in which you can change these behaviours.

The importance of behaviours

Behaviours, the things that you engage in which are related to your eating disorder (for example, strict dieting, frequent weighing, excessive exercise) are particularly important in maintaining negative thoughts about weight and shape.

Typical behaviours

We have identified the main behaviours, related to bulimia nervosa, in which people typically engage. A list of the categories of behaviours, with examples of the behaviours and catastrophe each is intended to prevent, can be seen in Box 14.1.

Linking behaviours with thoughts

If you are unconvinced by the idea that certain behaviours keep your negative thoughts about your weight and shape alive, try the following experiment.

Experiment

To see whether engaging in certain behaviours intensifies negative thoughts about weight and shape try gazing at your body in a full-length mirror for several minutes. Rate how anxious you feel about your weight and shape before doing this and then immediately afterwards. Use a 0–100% scale, with 0 being 'not at all anxious' and 100 being 'extremely anxious'. Then compare your ratings, particularly the after rating, with how anxious you feel about your weight and shape before and after describing an object outside your body.

Box 14.1 Behaviours and the catastrophe they are designed to prevent

Behaviours	Catastrophe
Dieting	
• Avoiding high calorie food	• If I eat this sort of food my stomach will become enormous
• Not eating before 6pm	• If I eat earlier in the day I'll overeat and gain weight
• Refusing sweets and cakes	• If I eat sugary foods I'll get fat
Weight and shape behaviour	
• Checking the size of your stomach	• If my stomach gets bigger I'll look bloated
• Measuring parts of your body	• If I start to get bigger I can cut down on my eating
• Wearing baggy clothes to conceal your shape	• If I wear tight-fitting clothes I'll look overweight
• Weighing yourself a lot	• If I keep a constant check on my weight I can take action
Food behaviour	
• Avoiding keeping a stock of food in the house	• If I keep food at home I'll be tempted to eat it – I'll get fat
• Memorising calorie values	• If I don't know the calorie value of foods I can't avoid those high in calories/avoid gaining weight

Mary did this experiment, gazing first at her reflection in a large mirror and then looking at and describing a bright picture on her bedroom wall. Her before and after ratings can be seen in Box 14.2.

Box 14.2 The results of Mary's experiment

Before gazing in the mirror Anxiety = 40%	**After gazing in the mirror** Anxiety = 85%
Before describing the picture Anxiety = 45%	**After describing the picture** Anxiety = 25%

As you can see, gazing at herself in the mirror increased her anxiety about her weight and shape, while describing the picture decreased it.

OUTCOME

After completing the experiment ask yourself, what do the results suggest? Can mirror gazing (a weight and shape related behaviour) increase your negative thoughts and your distress about your weight and shape. Mary concluded that it could.

Questionnaire to identify behaviours in which you engage

Questionnaire 14.1 will help you to identify which of the behaviours listed in Box 14.2 you engage in.

Questionnaire 14.1 Behaviours questionnaire

Instructions

Listed below are some statements about different behaviours. They all describe ways in which people sometimes behave. Please read each statement carefully and decide how often you find yourself behaving in the way described. Use the rating scale to describe how often you engage in each behaviour.

Rating scale

0   10   20   30   40   50   60   70   80   90   100

Never   Always

Questions

Dieting

1. ...... Avoid fats, carbohydrates and sugary food.

2. ...... Divide foods into good and bad or safe and unsafe foods.

3. ...... Check the calorie content of food before I buy it.

4. ...... Make rules about what I should or shouldn't eat.

5. ...... Try not to eat much during the day.

6. ...... Set myself a strict calorie limit for each day.

7. ...... Eat only 'safe' foods (i.e. low calorie or familiar foods).

8. ...... Avoid food if I don't know how many calories are in it.

9. ...... Try to deprive myself of food when I'm hungry.

10. ...... Try to control how much or what I'm eating.

11. ...... Eat diet foods.

Weight and shape

1. ...... Avoid weighing myself or, alternatively, weigh myself several times a day.

2. ...... Avoid looking at my body in the mirror or, alternatively, check it several times a day.

3. ...... Measure parts of my body.

4. ...... Check specific parts of my body to see if they are getting fatter or thinner.

5. ...... Exercise to lose weight or prevent weight gain.

6. ...... Diet to lose weight or prevent weight gain.

7. ...... Compare my weight and shape to those of other people.

8. ...... Avoid communal changing rooms.

9. ...... Avoid wearing tight fitting clothes.

10. ...... Avoid swimming.

11. ...... Wear baggy clothes that hide my shape.

Food

1. ...... Prepare all my own food.

2. ...... Weigh food before eating it.

3. ...... Hoard food.

4. ...... Read cookery books.

5. ...... Collect recipes.

6. ...... Talk about food.

7. ...... Eat as little as possible in front of other people.

8. ...... Avoid social situations where I know there will be food.

9. ...... When eating with others, try to eat less than they do.

10. ...... Cook for others but eat only a little of what I've prepared.

11. ...... Try to finish my meal last.

12. ...... Take the smallest portion when food is served.

Meaning of scores obtained on the questionnaire

To find out which types of behaviours you most frequently engage in, add up your scores for the three subscales separately and divide the total by the number of items in the subscale. For the first two subscales divide by 11. For the third subscale divide by 12. Record your scores on Worksheet 14.1.

Worksheet 14.1 Recording scores on the Behaviours Questionnaire

Subscale	Score
Dieting	
Weight and shape	
Food	

Scores on each sub-scale can be interpreted as shown in Box 14.3. The higher the score the more the behaviours on that sub-scale are likely to be a problem for you.

Box 14.3 Meaning of scores on the Behaviours Questionnaire

0–9   Low score. Unlikely to be much of a problem for you.

10–29   Moderate score. Likely to be somewhat of a problem for you.

30–59   High score. Likely to be quite a big problem for you.

60–100 Very high score. Likely to be a very big problem for you.

Fears about changing behaviours

Giving up these behaviours means that you will probably stop thinking so much about your weight and shape. Despite this, giving them up may not be easy. You probably feel quite anxious at the thought of what might happen. We touched upon a very common fear in Chapter 5 that giving them up will itself result in weight gain.

Catriona believed that if she stopped weighing herself several times a day then she would gain weight. Annie believed that if she stopped dieting (in her case, stopped having lots of rigid and complex rules about what she was allowed to eat), then she would eat whatever she felt like, without any limits. In the end this would mean that she would get fat. It is important to identify these sorts of fears so that you can challenge them and prevent them from sabotaging your attempts to give up the problematic behaviours. See Box 14.4 for some of the advantages of giving them up.

Box 14.4 Advantages of giving up behaviours maintaining negative thoughts

- Holding on to them prevents you from finding out what really happens – do you really gain weight or get fat if you give them up?

- It prevents you from developing better coping strategies – often they are ways to deal with distress and negative thoughts about yourself – giving them up will clear space to deal with these deeper level beliefs about yourself (see later chapters) in better ways.

Exercise: Identifying fears about giving up behaviours

Although there are some fears about giving up these behaviours that are shared by many people, other fears may be quite personal to you. It is important to identify what your own fears are. To help you do this, return to the Behaviours Questionnaire. Take each sub-scale that you have scored more than 30 on in turn and ask yourself: what would happen if I stopped behaving like this? Use Worksheet 14.2 to record each of the fears you identify.

Worksheet 14.2 Fears about giving up the behaviours that maintain negative thoughts

Dieting behaviour
Fear:

Weight and shape related behaviour
Fear:

Food related behaviour
Fear:

It is quite possible, but not always so, that you will find that your fears about giving up these behaviours and thinking processes are rather similar in each case. Leah scored above 30 on each subscale of the behaviours questionnaire (this is not uncommon). Take a look at Box 14.5 for examples of the types of different behaviours she engaged in and the fears she had about giving them up.

Box 14.5 Leah's fears about giving up problem behaviours

Dieting behaviour – e.g. dividing food into good and safe, bad and unsafe.

Fear: I'll gain weight, get fat and blobby; I'll have to think about all my other problems if I give up dieting.

Weight and shape related behaviour – e.g. weighing myself three times a day.

Fear: Unless I check my weight constantly, it will go up.

Food related behaviour – e.g. not eating with other people.

Fear: Eating normally with other people will draw attention to me. They'll think 'she's fat, she shouldn't be eating so much'.

If you look carefully at Leah's fears you'll notice that most of them focus on a fear of getting fat or gaining weight. This is quite common. However, notice that at least one of them reflects a fear of having to face all her other problems. This is also common.

Planning graded behavioural experiments to test fears

You have already devised some graded experiments to test out your thoughts of no control, now we suggest that you do the same to test out the fears you have about giving up the behaviours that keep your negative thoughts about weight and shape alive. Changing your behaviour and thinking styles gradually, step by step, in a series of behavioural experiments, will allow you to test out these fears and see whether, in practice, your fear was realistic.

Exercise: Planning your own behavioural experiments to test fears

There are probably a variety of behaviours maintaining your negative thoughts about your weight and shape. Choose the ones you do most frequently, making sure that you select a range from the different categories you scored on in the behaviours questionnaire. Then use the behavioural experiment worksheet introduced in Chapter 9 (see Worksheet 14.3) to help you plan a series of experiments to test out the main fear you have about giving up each behaviour.

Worksheet 14.3 Planning and recording behavioural experiments to test fears about giving up behaviours

Thought to be tested:

Belief that the thought is true (0–100%):

Experiment to test thought	Likely problems	Strategies to deal with problems	Date of experiment	Outcome of experiment	Belief in thought (0–100%)

Use Worksheet 14.3 to record the belief you are testing, for example, that you will gain weight if you stop weighing yourself several times a day, together with details of the experiments, as you plan and carry them out. Follow the instructions below for each experiment you plan.

Step 1

Write the fear about giving up the behaviour, in your own words, at the top of the sheet. Make sure you write down the worst that you think could happen.

Step 2

Rate your belief that the fear will come true on a 0 to 100% scale, with 0 being 'I do not believe this thought at all' and 100 being 'I am completely convinced that this thought is true'.

Step 3

Write what you plan to do to test out the fear in the left hand column under 'experiment to test thought'.

Step 4

To increase your chances of success think about any likely problems, for example, feeling tempted to weigh yourself as much as usual, and write these down under 'likely problems'.

Step 5

Under 'strategies to deal with problems' write down how you will deal with these problems if they arise.

Step 6

Carry out the experiment. When you have carried out the experiment, record the date of the experiment and brief details of the outcome.

Step 7

Finally, re-rate your belief in the original thought or fear.

Remember to start with behaviours that seem relatively easy to give up. Remember too that if the behaviour seems very difficult to give up then think how you can break it down into a series of smaller and easier steps. Plan to carry out the easier steps first.

Emily found it easier to give up her dieting and food-related behaviours before moving on to her weight and shape-related behaviours. She began by gradually eating more during the day. Then she increased the range of foods she was eating in small steps, followed by introducing foods which she normally only ate during a

Box 14.6 Emily's diet related experiment

Thought to be tested: If I eat normally (i.e. no diet foods), I'll get fat

Belief that the thought is true (0–100%): 80%

Experiment to test thought	Likely problems	Strategies to deal with problems	Date of experiment	Outcome of experiment	Belief in thought (0–100%)
Eat normal yoghurt instead of diet yoghurt for lunch	I'll be tempted to take diet yoghurt to work	Buy normal yoghurt instead of diet yoghurt when I go shopping so that there won't be any diet yoghurts in the 'fridge	Tuesday, 25th October	Managed to eat normal yoghurt with my lunch. Weighed myself next morning – I was two pounds heavier than the day before. Used my thought challenging skills. One pound does not equal fat – it's a normal fluctuation. Fat would be gaining much more than this.	40%

binge. She then started to eat in more social situations rather than only in private. Having successfully dealt with these, she moved on to her weight and shape behaviours, breaking them up into small steps and tackling them one step at a time in the same way. One of her dieting related experiments can be seen in Box 14.6.

Remember too that if the behaviour seems very difficult to give up, then think how you can break it down into a series of smaller and easier steps. Plan to carry out the easier steps first.

As before, don't despair if the experiment does not go well: it simply means that you need to revise it. Ask yourself three of the questions we introduced in Chapter 9 to find out where the problem was and then plan a revised experiment. These questions can be seen in Box 14.7.

Box 14.7 Questions to identify problems in behavioural experiments

- What did I learn from this?

- Was the task too difficult?

- Am I expecting too much of myself?

If your fears are all rather similar then you may find as you work through several experiments that any remaining fears also disappear and do not need to be tested separately. If your fears are all rather different then you will probably need to work through all of them.

Useful behavioural experiments

In Box 14.8 to get you started, are some ideas for experiments, based on those our patients have conducted.

A NOTE ABOUT 'GETTING FAT'

Many fears, like Emily's in Box 14.6, will involve a fear of getting fat or gaining weight. It is important that you are clear about what getting fat would involve. Emily appeared to gain two pounds – it would have been easy for her to interpret this as evidence that her fear was real. Instead she asked herself the questions in Box 14.9.

Having done this, Emily concluded that weighing an extra stone would be approaching getting fat, but that gaining two pounds most probably represented a normal weight fluctuation.

Box 14.8 Ideas for behavioural experiments

Dieting behaviour

- Introduce an unsafe food, e.g. a mini Mars bar, chocolate biscuit.

- Compare a day of restricting with a day of not restricting your food intake.

- Compare a day (or week) of checking calorie values with a day (or week) of not checking them.

- Compare a day of eating diet foods with a day of eating normal foods.

Weight and shape related behaviour

- Compare weighing yourself several times a day with weighing yourself once a week.

- Compare checking parts of your body several times a day with a day of not doing this at all.

- Go swimming.

- Go shopping and try on clothes.

- Wear a tight-fitting dress to a party.

- Compare an ordinary day (in which you focus on your stomach repeatedly) with a day in which you distract yourself when tempted to do so.

- Compare a day of gazing at yourself in mirrors, shop windows, etc. with a day of not doing this.

Food related behaviour

- Let your partner make his favourite meal (for both of you) for dinner.

- Stop buying and reading cookery books.

- Stop buying unnecessary food 'just in case'.

- Have a small portion of dessert when out for dinner.

- Order pasta in a restaurant.

Box 14.9 'Getting fat' fears

- What would getting fat mean?

- How would I know when I was fat?

- Is gaining a pound or two the same as 'getting fat?'

- What would my best friend say 'getting fat' was?

A NOTE ABOUT WEIGHT GAIN

Very, very occasionally, people find that they gain ten or more pounds when they give up bingeing and start eating normally. This does not make it easy to stick to the programme. It usually happens when they have been trying to maintain a weight well below their natural weight. You may remember that we touched upon this in Chapter 5. It may mean that to eat normally, without dieting you have to accept a weight rather higher than you might initially like. If this happens to you, and makes you think of abandoning the programme, go back to the exercises you completed in Chapters 5 and 6 and remind yourself of the long term benefits of overcoming bulimia nervosa.

Summary exercise

Write a brief summary of what you have learned from this chapter; both from the information presented and from the exercises. Also write down how you will put what you have learned into practice. Then write the essence of your summary and plans on a small index card. Put this in a bag or inside a diary that you usually carry with you and make time, twice a day, to read the card.

Chapter summary

This chapter has helped you identify the behaviours that may be keeping your negative thoughts about your weight and shape going. It also suggested ways to decrease these behaviours. The following important points were made:

- Negative thoughts about your weight and shape are maintained by certain behaviours.

- There are three types of behaviour – dieting, weight and shape related behaviour and food related behaviour.

- The Behaviours Questionnaire helps you to identify each type of behaviour.

- To decrease negative thoughts about weight and shape, you will need to give up some of your behaviours.

- Giving them up is not easy. A common fear is that giving them up will in itself lead to weight gain.

- Behavioural experiments can be used to test fears and, in the process, will decrease negative thoughts.

The following suggestions were made:

- Use the Behaviours Questionnaire to identify the behaviours that may be maintaining your negative thoughts about your weight and shape.

- Carry out an experiment to confirm the role of behaviours in maintaining these negative thoughts.

- Identify any fears you may have about giving up your behaviours.

- Use behavioural experiments to test out fears and, in the process, to decrease negative thoughts.

CHAPTER 15

Identifying Underlying Assumptions

Assumptions about weight and shape are extremely important in bulimia nervosa. They underlie all the thoughts that you learned how to identify and challenge in earlier chapters. They also underlie the behaviours, including both bingeing and vomiting as well as other behaviours such as frequent weighing and mirror gazing. They are particularly important because it is generally believed that, if they are not tackled, then relapse is highly likely. In this chapter we will explain what underlying assumptions are and how they link to thoughts and behaviour (particularly eating). We will then introduce you to three ways to identify them.

The nature of underlying assumptions about weight and shape

In bulimia nervosa assumptions about weight and shape typically concern what it means to the person to be fat or thin, or to gain or lose weight. They are often expressed in the form of 'if…then' statements. Usually, some assumptions will concern what being fat or thin would mean about the person herself, while others will concern what the person believes others would think of her if she were to become fat or thin. Examples of both types can be seen in Box 15.1.

Negative assumptions

Being fat or gaining weight is usually associated with a negative outcome. The person predicts that something bad or unpleasant will happen to her if she gains weight. Identifying your assumptions will help you to make sense of your eating disorder. If you believe that weight gain will have terrible consequences, then no wonder you are extremely concerned about your weight and shape and anxious to control it; no wonder you try hard to prevent weight gain.

Positive assumptions

In addition to negative assumptions about weight and shape, there are usually positive assumptions as well. These concern what it means to be thin or to lose weight. They are often the opposite of what it means to be fat. They suggest that there are positive benefits to be gained from being thin or from losing weight. These beliefs explain why people with eating disorders are often desperate to lose weight, and not just keen to prevent weight gain. See if you can work out which are the positive and which are the negative assumptions in Box 15.1.

Box 15.1 Examples of underlying assumptions about weight and shape

About yourself

- If I'm fat then I've failed.
- If I'm thin then I'm successful.
- If I gain weight then I'm no good.
- If I lose weight then I'm a better/more worthwhile person.
- If I gain weight I'm out of control.
- If I'm thinner I'll be more desirable.

About others

- If I gain weight then no one will like me/love me.
- If I lose weight then people will care more about me.
- If I get fat then other people will despise me.
- If I get thinner then others will take me more seriously.
- If I'm fat then I'm less acceptable to others.
- If I'm thin, others are more likely to think I'm ok/a good person.

Eating-related assumptions

As well as weight- and shape- related assumptions, people with eating disorders sometimes have assumptions about eating. These are typically concerned with what it means to eat or not to eat. At a very simple level, to many people with eating disorders, eating means they will get fat or gain weight; while not eating means that this is unlikely to happen. These beliefs are important. However, the eating assumptions that place you at risk of relapse are those concerned with what eating means about you, and with what you believe others will think of you if you eat. As with weight and shape assumptions, eating assumptions are of two kinds: those about yourself and those about others. They can also be negative or positive. Examples can be seen in Box 15.2. See if you can identify which are positive and which are negative.

Box 15.2 Examples of eating-related assumptions

About you

- If I eat then it means I've failed.
- If I can eat less then it means I'm in control.
- If I eat too much then it means I'm worthless.
- If I diet/don't eat then it means I'm virtuous.
- If I cut down on my food intake then I'm a good person.
- If I eat more than 1000 calories a day then I'm despicable.

About others

- If I eat in front of others they'll think I'm greedy.
- If I eat less others will think more of me.
- If I eat pasta and potatoes other people will think I don't have any willpower.
- If I refuse puddings and sweets, others will think I'm strong.
- If I eat too much others will think I've failed.
- If I eat less than others then they'll have more respect for me.

The relationship between underlying assumptions, thoughts and behaviour

Assumptions are often called 'underlying' assumptions. They are at a deeper level than thoughts. They underlie your problematic vicious circle thoughts, as well as your negative thoughts about weight and shape, and any behaviours you engage in that are related to your eating disorder. They are, in practice, the source of all these thoughts and behaviours. As suggested above, unless they are identified and challenged, then you will probably remain vulnerable to another episode of bulimia nervosa or, indeed, may develop another type of eating disorder.

Different types of underlying assumptions

There are two types of underlying assumptions about weight and shape in bulimia nervosa: the first focuses on self-acceptance; the second on acceptance by other people. Assumptions about eating can also be divided up into those that focus on self-acceptance and those that focus on acceptance by other people. Examples of all four can be seen in Box 15.3.

Box 15.3 Different types of underlying assumptions

Weight and shape – self acceptance

- If I'm thin then I'll be happy and successful.
- If my body is lean then I can feel good about myself – loveable and likeable.

Weight and shape – acceptance by others

- If my stomach is flat, I'll be more desirable to others.
- If my body is in proportion and slim then I'll be more popular.

Eating – self acceptance

- If I eat only fruit and vegetables then I'm virtuous.
- If I cut out fat, sugar and carbohydrates I'm a better/good person.

Eating – acceptance by others

- If I don't eat others will think I'm strong.
- If I refuse cakes and biscuits others will think I've lots of willpower/self control.

Techniques to identify underlying assumptions

Assumptions can be identified in three main ways:

- from themes in your thoughts records and from fears tested in behavioural experiments;
- by completing the two weight and shape subscales of the eating disorder belief questionnaire;
- by using a 'downward arrow' technique.

Identifying themes from thoughts records and from fears tested in behavioural experiments

Underlying assumptions can sometimes be identified quite easily from themes in your thoughts records or from themes in the fears you have tested in behavioural experiments. The procedure is simple. Select some representative examples of your thoughts records and behavioural experiment records. Then read them through carefully and see if you can find clues as to what your assumptions might be; that is, what it means to you to be fat or thin, or to eat or not eat.

Natalie noticed that she had four repeated thoughts. After examining them she came to the conclusion that she believed 'If my body is lean, I'll feel good about myself' and 'If my body is lean I'll be more desirable'. Look both for assumptions related to weight and shape and for assumptions related to eating. Check whether you have assumptions (of both kinds) that concern self-acceptance and assumptions that concern acceptance by others. Natalie's assumptions concerned both self-acceptance and acceptance by others.

Completion of the eating disorder belief questionnaire weight and shape subscales

Completing the eating disorder belief questionnaire weight and shape sub-scales (see Questionnaire 15.1) will help you to identify whether you have weight and shape assumptions focused on self-acceptance and on acceptance by others. Follow the instructions on the questionnaire carefully. It is important that you respond according to how you generally feel and not simply according to how you feel at the moment you complete it.

Interpreting scores on the questionnaire

To determine the strength of your assumptions in the two areas, add up your scores on each item. Do this separately for the two subscales so that you have two totals: one for assumptions about weight and shape as a means to self-acceptance; and one for assumptions about weight and shape as a means to acceptance by others. Divide each total by the number of questions on the corresponding subscale (self-acceptance subscale 6; acceptance by others subscale 10). Although people with eating disorders usually score highly on both subscales, it may be that one is relatively more important than the other in your own case. If this is so, then it will give you an idea of where you will need to focus your energies when it comes to challenging your idiosyncratic assumptions. Sunita found that both subscales were important to her, but that she scored significantly higher on the self-acceptance subscale. She chose to work on these assumptions first.

The downward arrow technique

This is, perhaps, the most effective way to identify your assumptions. Most importantly, it will enable them to be captured in your own words. The downward arrow technique works backwards from the last time you felt bad about your eating; it consists of a series of questions that are repeated over and over until an assumption in the form of an 'if…then' statement is identified. More specifically, it works backwards from your behaviour (eating), feelings and thoughts when you last felt upset or bad about your eating. This means that it will almost certainly capture your key assumptions; in particular, those that may make you vulnerable to relapse. Indeed, the

Questionnaire 15.1 Assumptions Questionnaire

Instructions

Below are a series of items. Read each item carefully. Then, choose a rating from the scale that best describes what you emotionally believe or feel, rather that what you rationally believe to be true. Choose the rating that best describes what you usually believe or what you believe most of the time. Write your rating in the space to the left of the item.

Rating Scale

0   10   20   30   40   50   60   70   80   90   100

I do not usually   I am usually
believe this at all   completely
                                                                    convinced

Self-acceptance

1. ...... If my stomach is flat I'll be more desirable.
2. ...... If my flesh is firm I'm more attractive.
3. ...... If my body is lean I can feel good about myself.
4. ...... If I eat desserts or puddings I'll get fat.
5. ...... Body fat/flabbiness is disgusting.
6. ...... If I eat bad foods such as fats, sweets, bread and cereals they will turn into fat.

Acceptance by others

1. ...... If my thighs are firm it means I'm a better person.
2. ...... If my hips are narrow it means I'm successful.
3. ...... If my bottom is small people will take me seriously.
4. ...... If I gain weight it means I'm a bad person.
5. ...... If I gain weight I'm nothing.
6. ...... If my body shape is in proportion people will love me.
7. ...... If my hips are thin people will approve of me.
8. ...... If I lose weight people will be friendly and want to get to know me.
9. ...... If I lose weight people will care about me.
10. ...... If I lose weight I'll count more in the world.

assumptions it identifies will probably be those that put you at risk of developing an eating disorder in the first place. Weight and shape and eating assumptions, focused on both self and other acceptance, can all be identified quite easily using this technique.

Exercise using the downward arrow technique to identify assumptions

Worksheet 15.1 will help you to identify your assumptions. Work through it, following the three steps and asking yourself all the questions.

Step 1

Start at the top with the question that asks you to identify the last time you felt bad about your eating. Make sure you pick an occasion that was not directly related to a binge. Then, once you have identified a suitable occasion, make sure that you spend sufficient time getting yourself back into the situation. Ask yourself what you can see, hear, feel (on your skin) and smell.

Identify the triggers and how you feel. Doing all this will help you pick up on the assumptions more easily. Go on to ask yourself whether you had any images, as well as thoughts, and what the thought in the image was.

Step 2

Then, pick the most salient of your thoughts to pursue using the downward arrow. The most salient thought should be the thought that distresses you most.

Step 3

Once you have identified this thought, ask yourself the downward arrow questions. The first two questions will identify assumptions related to self-acceptance and the second two will identify assumptions related to acceptance by others. Repeat these questions as necessary to identify all your assumptions. If your most distressing thought yields some eating related assumptions then make sure you check whether you also have any weight and shape assumptions by picking a distressing thought about your weight and shape and asking yourself exactly the same downward arrow questions about it.

After completing this exercise you should have identified your own idiosyncratic assumptions. You will not necessarily have assumptions in each of the categories mentioned in this chapter, but if you do then this exercise should have identified them for you. Look at Laura's completed worksheet in Box 15.4 to help you with this exercise.

Worksheet 15.1 Using the downward arrow technique to identify assumptions

Step 1: Setting the scene

- When was the last time that you felt really worried, anxious or bad about your eating (not a binge episode)?

Imagine that situation.

- What do you see, hear, feel (on your skin), smell?

- What were the triggers?

- How do you feel?

- What thoughts do you have?

- What images/pictures do you have?

- What thoughts do you have in the images?

Step 2: Identify the most distressing thought

- Which is the most distressing thought?

Step 3: Downward arrow questions

To identify assumptions related to self-acceptance:

- What would that mean about you or say about you?

- What's the worst that it could mean or say about you?

The assumption I hold is:

To identify assumptions related to acceptance by others:

- What do you think other people would think about you or do to you?

- What's the worst that they could think or do?

The assumption I hold is:

Box 15.4 Laura's completed worksheet: Identifying assumptions

Step 1: Setting the scene

- When was the last time that you felt really worried, anxious or bad about your eating (not a binge episode)?

A week ago. I felt disappointed with myself for eating a pudding.

Imagine that situation.

- What do you see, hear, feel (on your skin), smell?

Felt fat and heavy.

- What were the triggers?

Worrying about having gained two pounds.

- How do you feel?

Disgust.

- What thoughts do you have?

I'll get fat. My clothes won't fit. I'm a giant blob.

- What images/pictures do you have?

Of myself with rolls of fat, unable to breathe or move freely.

- What thoughts do you have in the images?

I'm huge, so fat.

Step 2: Identify the most distressing thought

- Which is the most distressing thought?

I'm so fat.

Step 3: Downward arrow questions

To identify assumptions related to self-acceptance:

- What would that mean about you or say about you?

I'd be less fit and agile.
I'd be unwise.
I wouldn't be doing well.
I'd be failing.

Box 15.4 continued

- What's the worst that it could mean or say about you?

That I was failing.

The assumption I hold is:

If I'm fat then I'm a failure.

To identify assumptions related to acceptance by others:

- What do you think other people would think about you or do to you?

They'd think I'm loud.

They'd laugh at me.

They'd notice me more – I'd be conspicuous.

They wouldn't accept me for myself – I wouldn't fit in.

They'd think me a fat and disgusting freak.

- What's the worst that they could think or do?

That they wouldn't accept me.

The assumption I hold is:

If I gain weight then I won't be accepted.

Summary exercise

Write a brief summary of what you have learned from this chapter; both from the information presented and from the exercises. Also write down how you will put what you have learned into practice. Then, write the essence of your summary and plans on a small index card. Put this in a bag or inside a diary that you usually carry with you and make time, twice a day, to read the card.

Chapter summary

This chapter has introduced you to underlying assumptions about weight, shape and eating. It has also shown you three ways to identify them. The following important points were made:

- Assumptions about weight and shape concern what it means to be fat or thin, or to gain or lose weight.
- Assumptions about eating concern what it means about you if you eat or don't eat.
- Assumptions can be negative or positive; positive assumptions are often the opposite of negative assumptions.

- Assumptions are at a deeper level than negative thoughts; they underlie these thoughts and behaviour.

- Unless assumptions are identified and challenged you will probably remain vulnerable to relapse or to another type of eating disorder.

- Assumptions are of two types: those focused on self-acceptance and those focused on acceptance by others.

It was suggested that you identify your assumptions using three strategies. These are listed below:

- Look for themes in thoughts records and in fears tested in behavioural experiments.

- Complete the weight and shape subscales of the eating disorder belief questionnaire.

- Work through the downward arrow technique; working backwards from a recent occasion on which you felt bad about your eating.

CHAPTER 16

Challenging Underlying Assumptions

In this chapter we will show you how to challenge your underlying assumptions. There are several ways to do this. We will introduce you to two of the strategies that our patients have found particularly helpful. In addition to challenging your assumptions we will also show you how to identify more helpful rules for living, and will suggest that you make plans to put these into practice in your everyday life. Finally, because assumptions generally reflect a person's goals in life, we suggest that you plan new ways to reach your goals.

Examining the advantages and disadvantages of assumptions

There are bound to be some advantages to continuing to believe in your assumptions about weight, shape and eating. If there weren't advantages then you would probably have given them up as a guide for living long ago. One of the most common and important advantages is that they provide a quick and easy way of measuring both your self worth and your value to other people. However, such assumptions are also likely to have certain disadvantages. In many cases, when people with bulimia nervosa examine the advantages and disadvantages in detail, they conclude that the disadvantages outweigh the advantages and that it is time to find some alternative guidelines for living.

Worksheet 16.1 Examining the advantages and disadvantages of assumptions

The assumption I hold is:

Belief in the assumption (0–100%):

Advantages	Disadvantages

Outcome:

Belief in the assumption now (0–100%):

Exercise to examine advantages and disadvantages

Use Worksheet 16.1 to challenge the assumptions you identified in Chapter 15, using a separate worksheet for each assumption. Follow the steps outlined below.

Step 1

Identify an assumption about yourself; in other words, what being fat and thin means or says about you. Write the assumption you want to challenge at the top of the worksheet and rate how much your usually believe it to be true. Use a 0 to 100% scale, with 0 being 'I do not usually believe this assumption at all' and 100 being 'I am usually completely convinced that this assumption is true'.

Step 2

Then, ask yourself what are the advantages of holding this belief and record all your answers on the worksheet under 'advantages'.

Step 3

When you have completed your response to this question, move on to disadvantages. Ask yourself what are the disadvantages of continuing to have this belief, and record all your answers under 'disadvantages'.

Step 4

When you have answered both questions, ask yourself what, on balance, your responses suggest about the usefulness of continuing to live your life according to this rule? Record your conclusions under 'outcome'.

Step 5

Finally, re-rate your belief in the assumption being challenged, using the same 0 to 100% scale.

Repeat this exercise for any further assumptions about yourself. You should also work through the exercise for any assumptions you have about what you think others will think of you if you are fat or thin, and for any eating related assumptions. To help you with this exercise take a look in Box 16.1 at Sabina's completed worksheet, in which she challenged the assumption 'if my body is lean and my stomach is flat then I'll be more desirable'.

Box 16.1 Sabina's completed worksheet: Challenging assumptions

The assumption I hold is: If my body is lean and my stomach is flat then I'll be more desirable

Belief in the assumption (0–100%): 70%

Advantages	Disadvantages
• Weight and shape provides a clear and easy way of calculating my self-worth (desirability). • When I'm losing weight then I feel very good about myself – likeable, attractive and desirable.	• It means constant dieting to keep my weight low and thus feel good. • It means vomiting, taking large amounts of laxatives, exercising for long periods. • It takes up lots of time. • It means I'm always thinking about food. • I end up constantly criticising myself – my looks, my shape, my weight – which drags me down.

Outcome: The assumption has some advantages as a guide for living, but there are many disadvantages to continuing to use it like this. I need to find other ways to feel good about myself (desirable) apart from my shape and how much I weigh.

Belief in the assumption now (0–100%): 25%

Because it is possible that you may be misinterpreting the evidence relevant to what others will think or do if you gain weight or eat, it may be helpful to include an additional question (see Worksheet 16.2). This is, what is the evidence against this assumption?

Otherwise, complete the exercise as before. Look in Box 16.2 at Kathryn's completed worksheet in which she challenged the assumption 'if I'm fat then I've failed'.

Worksheet 16.2 Examining the evidence for and against and disadvantages of assumptions

The assumption I hold is:

Belief in the assumption (0–100%):	

Evidence against:

Advantages	**Disadvantages**

Outcome:

Belief in the assumption now (0–100%):

Box 16.2 Kathryn's completed worksheet: challenging assumptions

The assumption I hold is: if I'm fat I've failed

Belief in the assumption (0–100%): 70%

Evidence against:

- Weight hasn't affected my ability to do well in life.
- Other people succeed regardless of weight – I can too.
- You can fail and be thin.
- I am likely to do less well if I'm losing weight, not looking after myself, and not eating properly.

Advantages	Disadvantages
• It gives me an excuse when I fail – I can blame my weight. • It's a protection against failure. • I don't have to think about why I really failed. • I don't have to think about all the other areas of my life that need attention.	• If I gain even a small amount of weight then I feel very bad indeed. • I forget my successes elsewhere. • It's a way of avoiding other problems (not helpful in the long term). • Hanging on to this belief is stopping me making progress in other areas.

Outcome: Fat is not necessarily the same as failure. Weight is not as important as I sometimes think. Holding on to this belief is not going to help me get better/make progress in areas that need attention.

Belief in the assumption now (0–100%): 25%

Identifying the origins of an assumption

It may be helpful to ask yourself where your assumptions come from. Assumptions about weight and shape and eating are usually acquired in childhood and early teenage years. They are often acquired before the young person has learned to question the values and attitudes of those around her. They may arise from the influence of parents and peers, or from cultural and media pressure on young girls and teenagers to be slim and attractive. This pressure is often accompanied by the implicit message that being slim and attractive is the route to happiness. Recognising where your assumptions come from may help you, as an older wiser adult, to distance yourself from them.

Exercise to identify the origins of assumptions

Ask yourself where each of your assumptions come from and use Worksheet 16.3 to record your responses. Use a separate worksheet for each assumption. Follow these steps.

Step 1

Write your assumption at the top of the worksheet and rate it on the same 0 to 100% scale, to indicate how much you believe it, that you used in the last exercise.

Step 2

Questions that will help you complete the exercise are written on the worksheet. They include asking where the assumption comes from; when you first remember thinking like this; what was happening in your life at the time.

Worksheet 16.3 Identifying the origins of an assumption

The assumption I hold is:

Belief in the assumption (0–100%):

Where did the assumption come from?

When did I first find myself thinking like this?

What was going on in my life at that time?

Conclusion:

Belief in the assumption now (0–100%):

You may find that most of your assumptions can be traced back to the same event or series of events in your early life. Alternatively, you may find that one experience or series of experiences explains your assumptions about yourself while another explains the assumptions you have about what you imagine others will think of you if you gain weight or eat. Take a look in Box 16.3 at Faith's completed worksheet to help you with this exercise.

Box 16.3 Faith's completed worksheet: Origins of assumptions

The assumption I hold is:

If I get fat, everyone will laugh at me.

Belief in the assumption (0–100%): 75%

Where did the assumption come from?

Being teased at school, called fatty, clumsy and four eyes.

When did I first find myself thinking like this?

Aged about 11 or 12. The first games lesson at my new secondary school, when we had to divide up into teams and no one picked me. Someone said I was too fat and clumsy to run and all the other girls laughed.

What was going on in my life at that time?

I'd just started a new school. It was quite a shock after the small cosy school I'd been at, and I was finding it difficult to settle in.

Conclusion:

It was cruel and unkind of my class to laugh at me and make fun of me. The teacher should have stepped in and stopped it, if not then, at least when it continued later on.

Belief in the assumption now (0–100%): 30%

Reinterpreting the past

After identifying the origins of your assumptions you may, as we suggested earlier, be able to reinterpret their meaning, as an older wiser adult looking back on the past. If you can do this follow these two additional steps.

Step 3

Write your conclusion, after considering your answers to all the questions and looking back as an older, wiser adult.

Step 4

Re-rate your belief in the assumption, using the same 0–100 scale.

However, this part of the exercise may not be so easy. If you find yourself unable to do this, ask yourself the additional questions in Box 16.4 and see if you can 'reframe' the past, that is find a balanced explanation for what happened to you. Having done this, re-rate your belief in the assumption on the 0–100% scale.

Box 16.4 Reframing the past

- What would I say to someone else who'd had that experience?

- What would I say to a child/young adult experiencing that now?

- What would my best friend say if I told her about it?

Identifying a more realistic or adaptive belief

By now you may well have concluded that your assumptions about weight, shape and eating are not particularly helpful to you. However, you will need something to put in their place; some alternative guidelines for living. Often, this involves two things: a decision to start using a wider range of qualities or experiences as a measure of your self-worth; and a re-evaluation of the interpretations you believe others make about your weight and shape.

Exercise: identifying a more realistic or adaptive belief

To develop one or more alternative assumptions, simply ask yourself what would be a more realistic or more helpful assumption to hold. Ava had initially held the belief 'if I'm fat others won't take me seriously'. She developed a new belief 'others will take me seriously, no matter what I weigh – being taken seriously depends on a range of other things that are more important than weight'. To help herself come up with this new belief Ava did two things. First she asked herself 'what would being taken seriously look like?' and 'how many of these attributes are true of me?' Next she made a list of all the things that would make a person take someone seriously, and asked herself 'to what extent does weight and shape figure in this list?'

Devising an action plan to put the new belief into practice

By now you should have formulated some new assumptions or new guidelines for living, particularly where your weight, shape and eating are concerned. To ensure that you do actually live according to these new assumptions or rules, it is usually helpful to decide on an action plan; ways in which you are going to make sure that you put your new beliefs into practice in your everyday life. Two strategies are usually helpful. First, it can be useful to write down on a small card (flashcard), exactly how you will put your new assumption into practice. Carry the flashcard around with you or put it somewhere you will see it regularly. Second, it can be useful to devise some behavioural experiments in which you deliberately act against your old belief and according to your new assumption or rule.

Exercise: devising an action plan

Your action plan should consist of both flashcards and behavioural experiments.

Flashcards

Completing a flashcard on which your new assumption is recorded is relatively easy. Just write the new assumption or rule for living on a piece of card. Blank or ruled index cards are particularly useful for this. Fridge magnets can then be used to display these cards in prominent places around the house, ensuring that you are frequently reminded of your new assumption.

Alternatively, carry the flashcards with you, remembering to get them out and read them at least once a day. You can see what Jennifer wrote on her flashcard in Box 16.5. The belief she had been challenging was 'if I'm fat then I can't feel good about myself'.

Box 16.5 Jennifer's flashcard

You'll never feel happy or good about yourself through trying to lose weight

---

Behavioural experiments

Behavioural experiments should also be planned to make sure that you do actually put your new rules for living into practice in your everyday life. You are probably skilled at devising these by now. As you have done before, plan a series of experiments, in which you will put your new assumption or rule into practice, perhaps in a graded way. Record details of what you plan to do and the outcome of any experiments using Worksheet 16.4.

Write the new assumption or rule that you plan to put into practice at the top of the worksheet. Record precisely what you plan to do, identify any potential problems and devise ways in which these might be overcome should they occur. When you

Worksheet 16.4 Planning and recording behavioural experiments to test assumptions

The assumption I hold is:

Belief that the assumption is true (0–100%):

Experiment to test assumption	Likely problems	Strategies to deal with problems	Date of experiment	Outcome of experiment	Belief in thought (0–100%)

Box 16.6 Celia's completed worksheet: A behavioural experiment to test an assumption

Assumption to be tested: If I eat a packet of crisps in front of my friend she'll think I'm selfish and greedy.

Belief that the assumption is true (0–100%): 65%

Experiment to test assumption	Likely problems	Strategies to deal with problems	Date of experiment	Outcome of experiment	Belief in thought (0–100%)
Eat a packet of crisps in front of Lucy. Ask 'Do you think I'm selfish and greedy keeping these all to myself?'	I'll feel too self-conscious and embarrassed to do it.	Remind myself that these are just feelings – not a reason not to do it. If I don't push myself a little I'll never find out if my fear is true and I'll never increase my confidence.	Monday, 5th June	Lucy said I wasn't being greedy.	25%

have carried out an experiment, record the date on which it was carried out, together with brief details of the outcome. You should also rate your belief in the new assumption or rule before and after completing each experiment, using a 0 to 100% scale, with 0 being 'I do not usually believe this at all' and 100 being 'I am usually completely convinced that this is true'.

If your initial idea for an experiment seems too ambitious, devise some easier steps so that you can gradually build up to the more difficult experiments. Remember, a negative outcome simply means that you need to ask yourself what went wrong and plan a revised experiment. In Box 16.6 you can see how Celia completed this worksheet.

Exploring new ways of achieving goals

Your weight, shape and eating assumptions will probably reflect some of your goals in life; for example, to feel good about yourself and be liked, valued and accepted by other people. These are universal goals. However, unlike many other people, you have probably been assuming that these goals can be achieved by losing weight or avoiding weight gain. Giving up weight loss as a route to happiness means that you will need to establish some new ways of achieving your goals.

Janine, like most people, wanted to be happy and feel accepted and valued. She made a list of all the things that would help her reach these goals. It included making new friendships at work, doing a night class in sculpture, accepting more party invitations and playing golf with her father.

Summary exercise

Write a brief summary of what you have learned from this chapter; both from the information presented and from the exercises. Also write down how you will put what you have learned into practice. Then, write the essence of your summary and plans on a small index card. Put this in a bag or inside a diary that you usually carry with you and make time, twice a day, to read the card.

Chapter summary

In this chapter we have introduced ways to challenge assumptions. The following important points were made:

- There are bound to be some advantages to continuing to believe in your weight, shape and eating related assumptions.
- When the advantages and disadvantages are considered, many people with bulimia nervosa conclude it is time to find some new rules for living.
- Assumptions are usually developed in childhood and early adolescence. Identifying their origins can help you achieve some distance from them.

- Several assumptions can sometimes be traced back to the same event or series of events.

- You will need some more realistic and helpful assumptions to replace your unhelpful ones.

- Assumptions will usually reflect your goals in life; giving up weight loss as a way to achieve your goals means that you will need new ways to achieve them.

The following suggestions were made:

- Challenge your assumptions by examining the advantages and disadvantages of continuing to hold them and by identifying their origins.

- Identify some more realistic or adaptive beliefs.

- Use flashcards and behavioural experiments to put your new assumptions into practice in your everyday life.

- Explore new ways of achieving your goals.

CHAPTER 17

Identifying Core Beliefs

In bulimia nervosa core beliefs about the self, sometimes referred to as negative self-beliefs, are usually very important. They underlie the assumptions that you learned how to identify and challenge in earlier chapters. Like underlying assumptions, if they are not tackled then relapse is more likely. In this chapter we explain what core beliefs are and how they link to underlying assumptions. We will then introduce three ways to identify them and a strategy to identify their origins.

The nature of core beliefs

Core beliefs include beliefs about other people and the world as well as negative self-beliefs. They are expressed as absolute statements. There are no qualifications to them, as there are in assumptions where the way lies open for things to improve if you behave in certain ways. In bulimia nervosa core beliefs about the self are usually more important than beliefs about other people or the world. Because of this we will focus on these in this and the next chapter. Examples of typical negative self-beliefs can be seen in Box 17.1.

Box 17.1 Typical negative self-beliefs

- I'm a failure.

- I'm no good.

- I'm useless.

- I'm all alone.

- I'm inadequate.

- I'm worthless.

Core beliefs are usually formed in early childhood and, even more so than assumptions, they tend to remain unquestioned. You probably accept your negative beliefs about yourself as part of you. Indeed, you may find it almost impossible to think of yourself differently. Cheryl accepted her belief 'I'm no good' as part of her make-up and could not imagine seeing herself any differently. However, just as you have learned to challenge thoughts and underlying assumptions, so you can learn how to challenge your negative self-beliefs. The first step, and the topic of this chapter, is to learn how to identify them.

Core beliefs and feelings

Core beliefs are usually accompanied by strong feelings. When they are activated you may feel very upset. It is important that you continue to practice the skills you have learned so far, to help you to manage any upsetting feelings, while you are carrying out the suggestions in this and the next chapter.

The relationship between core beliefs and assumptions

In cognitive theory, core beliefs are the deepest level of thoughts that we have. They are at a deeper level than assumptions, which lie in between negative thoughts (those in the bingeing vicious circle, and those related to weight and shape) and core beliefs. The relationship between negative thoughts, underlying assumptions and core beliefs is illustrated in Figure 17.1.

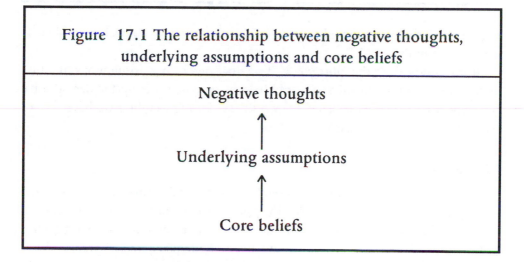

Figure 17.1 The relationship between negative thoughts, underlying assumptions and core beliefs

Negative thoughts

↑

Underlying assumptions

↑

Core beliefs

Assumptions often provide a means of overcoming one or more core beliefs (see Eva's example). However, negative self-beliefs reflect a belief that, at the end of the day, the person is truly, for example, unloveable, unlikeable or worthless. The relationship

---

Figure 17.2 Eva's thoughts, assumptions and negative self-beliefs

Negative thoughts

I've got to eat less
I must lose weight
I'm getting fat

↑

Underlying assumptions

If I lose weight I'm more worthwhile
If I eat too much I'm a bad/useless person

↑

Core beliefs

I'm useless
I'm a failure
I'm worthless

---

between Eva's negative thoughts, underlying assumptions and negative self-beliefs can be seen in Figure 17.2.

If you study Eva's thoughts you will see that one of her assumptions 'if I lose weight I'm more worthwhile' is a way to overcome or make up for her negative self-beliefs, particularly the belief 'I'm worthless'. Losing weight gives her a way to feel much better about herself.

Identifying core beliefs

Core beliefs can be identified in several ways. We will introduce you to three strategies that will help you to identify your negative core beliefs: completing a subscale of the eating disorder belief questionnaire, completing a brief sentence completion task and using the downward arrow technique. As we emphasised with negative thoughts and underlying assumptions, it is important to work out exactly what your core beliefs are before you start to challenge them.

Completing the negative self-beliefs subscale of the eating disorder belief questionnaire

In Chapter 15 you used two of the subscales of the eating disorder belief question-naire (Questionnaire 15.1) to help you identify underlying assumptions related to your weight and shape. The questionnaire has another subscale: the negative self-beliefs subscale (see Questionnaire 17.1). This will help you to determine the extent to which negative self-beliefs (core beliefs about the self) are a problem for

---

Questionnaire 17.1 Core beliefs questionnaire

Instructions

Below are a series of items. Read each item carefully. Then, choose a rating from the scale that best describes what you emotionally believe or feel, rather than what you rationally believe to be true. Choose the rating that best describes what you usually believe or what you believe most of the time. Write your rating in the space to the left of the item.

Rating scale

0   10   20   30   40   50   60   70   80   90   100

I do not   I am usually
usually believe   completely
this at all   convinced that

Questions

1. ...... I'm stupid.
2. ...... I'm no good.
3. ...... I'm a failure.
4. ...... I'm useless.
5. ...... I'm dull.
6. ...... I'm not a likeable person.
7. ...... I'm all alone.
8. ...... I don't like myself very much.
9. ...... I'm unloveable.
10. ...... I'm ugly.

you. Follow the instructions at the top of the scale and complete the belief ratings for each item.

Meaning of scores obtained

To obtain an overall score of the extent to which you hold absolute, negative beliefs about yourself, add up the ratings given to each question and divide the total by ten. This will give you an average or mean score. In people with eating disorders this is generally quite high. A score above 60 is not uncommon.

Completing the sentence completion test

The sentence completion test is a quick and simple way to identify key negative self-beliefs. It asks you to write the first thing that comes to mind in response to the incomplete sentence, 'I am...'. Three incomplete sentences can be seen in Worksheet 17.1.

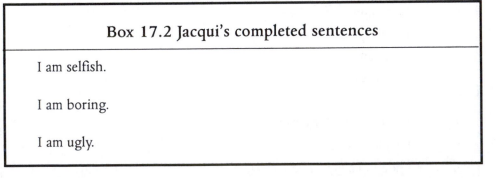

Worksheet 17.1 The sentence completion task

I am ....

I am ....

I am ....

Write your response to each sentence. In Box 17.2 you can see what Jacqui wrote to complete the three sentences.

Box 17.2 Jacqui's completed sentences

I am selfish.

I am boring.

I am ugly.

Occasionally, people write 'I'm fat'. Strictly speaking this is not a core belief: rather it is a negative thought (at a rather lower level, see Figure 17.1). This is because if you ask yourself the downward arrow questions 'What does this mean or say about me?', you will find you arrive at a deeper (true core belief) level. 'I'm fat' is not the bottom line.

Meaning of responses recorded

The completed 'I am...' sentence will help you to identify your key beliefs about yourself. In particular, it will help you to identify any beliefs not on the questionnaire. As we have suggested, and like Jacqui's beliefs, these will often be very negative.

Using the downward arrow technique

In Chapter 15 we introduced you to the downward arrow technique, which you used to identify your underlying assumptions. This technique can also be used to identify any remaining negative self-beliefs. Because core beliefs underlie assumptions, just as assumptions underlie negative thoughts, you can identify your negative self-beliefs by continuing to ask the questions (about yourself) that you initially asked of your negative thoughts in Chapter 15.

Exercise: Using the downward arrow technique to identify core beliefs

To use the downward arrow technique to identify negative self-beliefs, return to the assumptions you identified in Chapter 15 and complete Worksheet 17.2. Follow the steps below.

Worksheet 17.2 Using the downward arrow technique to identify core beliefs

To identify negative self-beliefs
Summarise assumptions about yourself:

Ask:

- What would that mean about you or say about you?

- What's the worst that it could mean or say about you?

Summarise negative self-beliefs:

Finally ask: Do the core beliefs you have identified reflect your general beliefs about yourself?

Step 1

Start by writing a summary of your assumptions about yourself.

Step 2

Then, ask yourself the questions on the worksheet, under 'to identify negative self-beliefs'. These will help you to identify your core beliefs about yourself. Repeat the two questions until you arrive at an absolute, unconditional belief about yourself. You will know you are there when it seems as if you are going round in circles, coming up with the same beliefs over and over again.

Step 3

Finally, check whether the beliefs you have identified reflect the way in which you usually see yourself.

Take a look in Box 17.3 at Maggie's completed worksheet to help you with this exercise. Maggie asked herself 'What would that mean or say about you?' twice. You may need to repeat the question a few more times than this in order to arrive at your own negative self-beliefs.

Meaning of responses identified

This exercise will have helped you to identify your key negative self-beliefs. As we have already noted, core beliefs about the self are invariably negative in eating disorders. The beliefs you have identified here will probably reflect this.

Identifying the origins of core beliefs

Sometimes it can be helpful to identify the origins of your core beliefs. Identifying their source can start to establish some distance from them. This can be helpful when you start to challenge them. It is important to remember, however, that what matters most of all now is how you deal with the beliefs you are left with. This will be covered in the next chapter.

The relationship between bingeing, dieting and core beliefs

Negative self-beliefs play a role in eating disorders. They help to trigger negative feelings, and then eating is used as a way to cope with negative thoughts and distressing feelings. They are also often related to dieting. To check whether and how bingeing and dieting are related to your own negative self-beliefs complete Worksheet 17.3. The question on this worksheet asks you to investigate whether and how bingeing and dieting help with your negative self-beliefs.

If you reported that you change your eating behaviour in response to the question on Worksheet 17.4 then your beliefs are probably related to your eating disorder. Usually, people with bulimia nervosa find that binge eating is a way to avoid any

Box 17.3 Maggie's completed worksheet: Identifying negative self-beliefs

To identify negative self-beliefs

Summarise assumptions about yourself:

If I'm fat I can't feel good about myself. My friends will despise me, they won't want to know me.

Ask:

- What would that mean about you or say about you?

I'll end up without any friends.

- What would that mean about you or say about you?

I'll be all by myself.

- What's the worst that it could mean or say about you?

I'll end up all alone.

Summarise negative self-beliefs:

I'm all alone.

Finally, ask: Do the core beliefs you have identified reflect your general beliefs about yourself?

Yes, this is how I generally think about myself.

Worksheet 17.3 Identifying the relationship between bingeing, dieting and negative self-beliefs

When you feel distressed and think I'm (summarise your negative self-beliefs) is there anything you could do or actually do to change how you feel or think?

Box 17.5 Lizzie's completed worksheet:
Linking bingeing, dieting and negative self-beliefs

When you feel distressed and think *'I'm ugly, pathetic, a loser, not worth anything'* (summarise your negative self-beliefs) is there anything you can do or actually do to change how you feel or think?

I can, and usually do, binge. Bingeing helps me escape from my negative thoughts and bad feelings.

Sometimes I decide to diet. Dieting is a way to feel better, less ugly, less pathetic, less of a loser. It's a way to feel worth something.

---

negative thoughts and feelings about themselves, while dieting is a way to overcome or make up for these thoughts and feelings. Lizzie believed that she was 'ugly, pathetic, a loser, not worth anything'. Her response to the question can be seen in Box 17.5.

Summary exercise

Write a brief summary of what you have learned from this chapter, both from the information presented and from the exercises. Also write down how you will put what you have learned into practice. Then, write the essence of your summary and plans on a small index card. Put this in a bag or inside a diary that you usually carry with you and make time, twice a day, to read the card.

Chapter summary

This chapter has introduced you to core beliefs, particularly negative self-beliefs. It has also shown you three ways to identify them, and introduced a strategy to identify their origins. The following important points were made:

- Core beliefs are expressed as absolute statements.
- They include beliefs about the self (negative self-beliefs), beliefs about other people and beliefs about the world.
- They are usually formed in early childhood and often remain unquestioned.
- Core beliefs are the deepest level of thought in cognitive theory. They are at a deeper level than assumptions.

- Core beliefs about the self are nearly always negative in bulimia nervosa. They are usually more important than core beliefs about other people and the world.

- Identifying the origins of your core beliefs can help you to establish some distance from them.

- Bingeing is often a way to avoid negative core beliefs about yourself and the feelings that go with these beliefs. Dieting is often a way to overcome or make up for them.

It was suggested that you identify your negative self-beliefs, using three strategies. These are listed below:

- Complete the negative self-beliefs subscale of the eating disorder belief questionnaire.

- Complete a brief sentence completion task.

- Use the downward arrow technique, working backwards from the assumptions you have identified.

CHAPTER 18

Challenging Core Beliefs

It is important to challenge your negative core beliefs, particularly your negative self-beliefs, so that you no longer believe so strongly that they are true. However, it is also important to build up new, more positive beliefs. In this chapter we will introduce you to a selection of strategies that will help you to challenge your old negative self-beliefs and build new, more positive beliefs.

The speed of change

Core beliefs do not usually change as quickly as negative thoughts or underlying assumptions. You should be prepared for them to change relatively slowly. The exercises in this chapter will need to be done over the course of several weeks, perhaps even months.

A long-term strategy

You should aim to return to each exercise in this chapter regularly, in order to build on it further. It is often a good idea to make an appointment with yourself once a week to review one or more exercises. This could be to add to them or expand on them (using evidence collected over the course of the week), or to make sure that you keep planning new ways, perhaps using behavioural experiments, to build up the new beliefs that you are developing.

Strategies and exercises to challenge beliefs

A variety of strategies and exercises can be used to challenge core beliefs. They include: the core belief worksheet, cognitive continua, historical tests of beliefs, positive data logs, behavioural experiments, and the development and use of flashcards. Each will be explained below.

Core belief worksheet

This strategy is one with which you are already familiar. It involves examining the evidence against negative core beliefs. In particular, it looks for any evidence that suggests they are not completely true all the time. It also takes examining the evidence a step further, and involves challenging the evidence you have that appears to support your old belief. A core belief worksheet (Worksheet 18.1) can be completed to challenge each of your negative self-beliefs in this way. We will talk you through completing it.

Worksheet 18.1 Core belief worksheet	
Old core belief:	
Belief in it now (0–100%):	
New core belief:	
Belief in it now (0–100%):	
Evidence that contradicts old core belief and supports new belief	**Evidence that supports old core belief with reframe**
Old core belief:	**New core belief:**
Belief in it now (0–100%):	**Belief in it now (0–100%):**

Step 1

Choose one of the negative self-beliefs that you identified in the last chapter.

Step 2

Write it at the top of the worksheet. Rate how much you believe it to be true, using a scale from 0 to 100%, with 0 being 'I do not believe this at all' and 100 being 'I am completely convinced that this is true'.

Step 3

You will then need to decide upon a new self-belief. Sometimes this will be the opposite of your old belief (e.g. 'I'm loveable' instead of 'I'm unloveable'). More commonly, it will be a qualified belief (e.g. 'I am a likeable person most of the time' instead of 'I'm unlikeable'). To help yourself find a new belief ask 'If I no longer believed that I was (old negative self-belief), how would I like to see myself?' Remember, the new belief must be realistic.

Step 4

Record your new belief on the worksheet and rate it on the same 0 to 100% scale that you used to rate your old belief. You will probably find that you believe it very little at first. Don't feel discouraged. This is quite normal.

Step 5

In the left-hand column of the worksheet, under 'evidence against', list all the evidence you have that your old belief is not completely true, together with any evidence which suggests that your new belief is true, even if only some of the time. Be careful when identifying evidence for your new belief. It is easy to ignore or discount relevant evidence. Try to notice and record even the smallest sign that it may be true.

Step 6

Then, in the other column, under 'evidence for', record any evidence you have that the old belief is true. However, instead of leaving this evidence unchallenged, use the questions in Box 18.1 to come up with an alternative perspective, a 'reframe' of the evidence.

Step 7

After doing this, re-rate your old and new beliefs.

Box 18.1 Reframing the past

- What's another way of interpreting this evidence?

- What would I say to someone else who'd had that experience?

- What would I say to a child/young adult experiencing that now?

- What would my best friend say if I told her about it?

Naomi (who came up with the new belief 'I can do many things perfectly well' as an alternative to her old belief 'I'm a failure') completed Worksheet 18.1 to assess her new belief. It can be seen in Box 18.2.

Box 18.2 Naomi's completed core belief worksheet

Old core belief: I'm a failure.

Belief in it now (0–100%): 90%

New belief: I can do many things perfectly well.

Belief in it now (0–100%): 20%

Evidence that contradicts old core belief and supports new belief	Evidence that supports old core belief with reframe
• Failing at something does not make me a failure as a person. • I can learn from my mistakes. • When Kerry criticised my appearance I was philosophical about it. • I'm resilient – when I argue with Gary now I don't take it to heart in the same way as I once did. • When I disagreed with Peter I didn't feel the need to prove myself inside, as I used to. • I'm more confident. • My appraisals of situations are more realistic.	• Got a low mark in an exam: reframe – what did I expect, I didn't study for it. My other marks are OK. • Not chosen for a part in a play: reframe – I can't be the best at everything, just because someone else was chosen doesn't make me a total failure.
Old core belief: I'm a failure.	**New core belief:** I can do many things perfectly well.
Belief in it now (0–100%): 50%	**Belief in it now (0–100%):** 60%

Your worksheet should evolve. Get it out as often as possible and add to it, using recently gathered evidence. Try gathering three pieces of evidence each day that support your new belief. Then, once a week, re-rate your old and new beliefs. As you do this, you will find belief in your old belief declines and belief in your new belief grows. After three months of working on her new and old beliefs in this way, Naomi believed 'I'm a failure' only 25% and 'I can do many things perfectly well' 85%.

Cognitive continua

These are a powerful way to challenge negative core beliefs and build up new, more positive beliefs. They use a single scale (a cognitive continuum) to measure the extent to which you believe both an old self-belief and the new belief you have generated to replace it. The scale runs from 0 to 100%, with 0 representing 'I do not believe this at all' and 100 representing 'I am completely convinced that this is true'. An example of a scale can be seen on Worksheet 18.2. We will talk you through using Worksheet 18.2.

Worksheet 18.2 Cognitive continua

0   10   20   30   40   50   60   70   80   90   100

Old belief   **New belief**

0   10   20   30   40   50   60   70   80   90   100

0   10   20   30   40   50   60   70   80   90   100

0   10   20   30   40   50   60   70   80   90   100

0   10   20   30   40   50   60   70   80   90   100

0   10   20   30   40   50   60   70   80   90   100

etc.

Step 1

On the left-hand side of the first scale write your old core (negative self) belief, and on the right-hand side write your new belief.

Step 2

Put a cross on the scale to indicate your current belief in the old and the new way of thinking (look at Marianne's example in Box 18.3 to help you with this).

Step 3

Putting aside all the evidence you have for and against your own beliefs at the moment, write down all the evidence you would use to decide that someone else was at the extreme left-hand end of the scale. Write one piece of evidence at the left-hand of each scale, working your way down the worksheet.

Step 4

Having done this, take each piece of evidence in turn and generate the opposite example of it; that is, evidence which you would use to decide that someone else was at the extreme right-hand end of the scale. Write each piece of evidence at the corresponding right-hand end of the scale. Remember, you are looking for signs that someone (not yourself) is at the two extremes. After doing this you will have a series of scales.

Step 5

Take each scale separately and rate where you fall on it, using a 0 to 100% rating, with 0 being 'does not describe me at all' and 100 being 'describes me completely'.

Step 6

Then, having done this for each of the scales that you created, revisit the old and new core belief ratings that you made at the top of the worksheet and, making a second cross on the scale, re-rate your belief in them now. Again, look at Marianne's example in Box 18.3 to help you with this.

On completing her worksheet Marianne was able to get a more balanced perspective on her self-belief and discovered that she had a higher level of likeable attributes than she had first believed.

Box 18.3 Marianne's completed worksheet: Cognitive continua

```
                X                       X
_____
0    10   20   30   40   50   60   70   80   90   100
Old belief                                   New belief
I'm unlikeable                               I'm likeable
```

```
                                   X
_____
0    10   20   30   40   50   60   70   80   90   100
No friends                         Popular, lots of friends
```

```
                                        X
_____
0    10   20   30   40   50   60   70   80   90   100
Never asked out                    Gets lots of invitations
                                   to go places
```

```
                    X
_____
0    10   20   30   40   50   60   70   80   90   100
No family                          Has good family
                                   relationships
```

```
                                   X
_____
0    10   20   30   40   50   60   70   80   90   100
Dresses like a bag lady            Is a cool dresser
```

```
                                        X
_____
0    10   20   30   40   50   60   70   80   90   100
Has rippling layers of fat,             Is attractive
no chin (like a turtle),
stomach down to the
knees, is smelly
```

```
                                             X
_____
0    10   20   30   40   50   60   70   80   90   100
Is completely isolated             Has lots of shared interests
(never does anything with others)  with others
```

```
                         X
_____
0    10   20   30   40   50   60   70   80   90   100
Refuses to go                      Is able to stay up
when asked                         all night at a rave
```

Box 18.3 continued

| X |
| 0   10   20   30   40   50   60   70   80   90   100 |

Is nasty and rude   Is friendly and helpful

| X |
| 0   10   20   30   40   50   60   70   80   90   100 |

Has extreme prejudices   Has balanced opinions
(e.g. believes all women are inferior)

| X |
| 0   10   20   30   40   50   60   70   80   90   100 |

Is mean and selfish   Is generous and kind
(e.g. always refuses to give to charity)

Historical tests of beliefs

This strategy asks you to review your life history to find examples of evidence, at different ages, that support your new core belief. It also asks you to identify evidence that is consistent with your old belief but, as with the core belief worksheet, instead of leaving this evidence unquestioned, use the questions in Box 18.2 to challenge it and record what, when challenged, the evidence now suggests (a reframe). Use Worksheet 18.3 to complete this exercise. Follow the steps below to complete this worksheet.

Step 1

Start by recording your old and new core beliefs, and how far you believe them to be true, using a 0–100% scale.

Step 2

Make a prediction about what you will find if you look over your lifetime.

Step 3

Then, identify evidence consistent with your old and new beliefs. Remember, don't accept the evidence consistent with your old belief without questioning it. Challenge (reframe) it using the questions in Box 18.1. Do this separately for each of the age bands; writing a brief summary of what the evidence in each age band suggests.

Worksheet 18.3 Historical test of beliefs

Old core belief:

New core belief:

Prediction if I look over my lifetime:

Age	Experiences I had that are consistent with the old core belief with reframe	Experiences I had that are consistent with the new core belief
0–2		

Summary:

3–5		

Summary:

6–12		

Summary:

13–18		

Summary:

19–25		

Summary:

26–35		

Summary:

36+		

Summary:

Overall summary:

Compare outcome of historical test of core belief to prediction:

Re-rate old and new core beliefs:

Old core belief (0–100%):

New core belief (0–100%):

Step 4

Finally, write an overall summary, answer the remaining questions and then, at the bottom of the worksheet, re-rate your old and new beliefs, using the 0 to 100% rating scale. In Box 18.4 you can see how Annette completed this worksheet. Note that she had the same negative self-belief as Naomi but her new core belief looked a little different.

Box 18.4 Annette's completed worksheet: Historical review of core belief

Old core belief: I'm a failure

New core belief: I can be successful at many things 25%

Prediction if I look over my lifetime: I will find I've failed at most things.

Age	Experiences I had that are consistent with the old core belief with reframe	Experiences I had that are consistent with the new core belief
0–2	I was slow to walk. **Reframe:** This seems to run in the family – I was no slower than my brothers.	I reached all my other developmental milestones on time or early. For example, I began to talk early.

Summary: I succeeded at all but one early developmental task, either on time or early.

3–5	I found it hard to start school. **Reframe:** Lots of children find this difficult. Once I'd settled in I did well.	I learned to read quickly. My class teacher gave me lots of praise for my drawings.

Summary: After a rather difficult start I did well with most things at school.

6–12	I fell out with my best friend. I found it hard to learn how to swim. I was bad at sports. **Reframe:** Girls fall out with their best friends all the time – we soon made up. Not everyone can be good at sports.	I continued to do well at school. I won a prize for my art work.

Summary: Not everyone can be good at everything. I was doing well in the things I enjoyed.

Box 18.4 continued

Age	Experiences I had that are consistent with the old core belief with reframe	Experiences I had that are consistent with the new core belief
13–18	I was shy with boys. Most of my friends had a boyfriend before I did. **Reframe:** When I was 17 I met Mark – we've been together three years – he was worth waiting for!	I continued to enjoy art. I got a place at art college. My parents said I'd done well and that they were proud of me.
Summary: Although it was hard to get on with boys at first I did eventually meet Mark (and we've stayed together). That's a success. Meanwhile I was still doing well at Art.		
19–25	Did badly in my first year college exams. **Reframe:** I hadn't worked hard enough – found it difficult to adjust to leaving home.	Did well in the next two years. Got a graphic design job in a prestigious company.
Summary: On the whole I enjoyed college and did well, after a rather difficult start.		
Overall summary: Looking back, I haven't succeeded at everything but I have succeeded at several things, particularly the things I enjoy. I've been particularly successful with my art work.		
Compare outcome of historical test of core belief to prediction: It's not true to say I've failed at most things.		
Re-rate old and new core beliefs: **Old core belief (0–100%):** I'm a failure 40% **New core belief (0–100%):** I can be successful at many things 50%		

This is another exercise that you can build on from week to week. As you develop this exercise and search for more evidence consistent with your new belief, you may find it helpful to talk to relatives and friends who knew you well at the different ages. Annette continued to add to her worksheet. After a further two months she believed 'I'm a failure' only 20% and 'I can be successful at many things' 75%.

Positive data logs

This is also a longer term strategy; one that can be built on from week to week. It is rather like keeping a daily diary. Get yourself a notebook, identify your new core beliefs and keep a log, every day, of all the experiences you have that are consistent with your new beliefs. Lots of these experiences may seem quite small or trivial, but all are important in building up your new beliefs. Remember to record facts and not interpretations. If you are worried that you won't find anything at all to write down then take a look in Box 18.5 for ideas about the sorts of things you might include.

Box 18.5 Ideas for your positive data log

- Things others say about you, e.g. praise, positive remarks, compliments.

- How others are with you, e.g. being warm and friendly, showing an interest in you, giving you gifts, cards, invitations.

- What you have done for yourself that was hard, e.g reading a book, making small changes, pampering yourself, being kind to yourself.

- What you have thought about yourself, e.g. challenging self-critical thoughts, thinking about yourself more positively, congratulating, complimenting yourself.

Try to set aside time at the end of each day to add to your log, and also to review and read your log regularly. Look in Box 18.6 for a page out of Monica's notebook. The new core beliefs she was building up were 'on the whole, I'm a likeable and worthwhile person'.

Box 18.6 Monica's positive data log

Steven said I had a good sense of humour.

I got a postcard from Judith.

I stood up for myself, instead of backing down and apologising – no one fell out with me over it.

Had a long bubble bath.

Complimented myself on my new hairstyle – it really suits me.

Behavioural experiments

You have already learned a great deal about behavioural experiments. They are a particularly useful way to test predictions based on your core beliefs. Use Worksheet 18.4 to plan these experiments.

Worksheet 18.4 Planning and recording behavioural experiments to test predictions based on core beliefs

Core belief to be tested:

Belief that the core belief is true (0–100%):

Experiment to test core belief	Likely problems	Strategies to deal with problems	Date of experiment	Outcome of experiment	Belief in core belief (0–100%)

Box 18.7 Hilary's completed worksheet: A behavioural experiment to test a new core belief

Core belief to be tested: I do fit in.

Belief that the core belief is true (0–100%): 20%

Experiment to test core belief	Likely problems	Strategies to deal with problems	Date of experiment	Outcome of experiment	Belief in core belief (0–100%)
Make a list of what 'fitting in' means. Go to the party at the weekend. Talk to five different people. Make a note of their reactions. Check these against what 'fitting in' means.	I won't know what to say to people. I'll have nothing in common with people there. No one will like me.	Remember, you can fit in without doing all the talking. Remember, you don't have to share everyone's interests all the time. Make and read a flashcard of 'reasons why I don't have to be liked by everyone'.	Saturday, 8th July	Enjoyed the party. Chatted with at least five people. Collected evidence for my positive data log – checked their reactions against 'what fitting in' means. Was pleasantly surprised to find I fitted in well with most of the people I'd talked to.	45%

It is usually most useful to plan experiments that will test the new belief that you are developing. After completing several experiments write a brief, general summary of what the outcomes suggest. It may be useful to put this summary in your positive data log.

Remember, a negative outcome is just as useful as a positive one. It is usually a sign that you need to revise your experiment. Work on doing this in the same way as you did before. Identify the problem and plan a new revised experiment based on what you have learned. Hilary devised an experiment to test her new belief 'I do fit in'. Her completed worksheet can be seen in Box 18.7.

Development and use of flashcards

You were introduced to flashcards in Chapter 16 as a means of recording and providing a quick and simple reminder of new assumptions. You can also use them to record your new core beliefs. Display the cards in prominent places around your home, or carry them with you, remembering to get them out and read them frequently.

Self-defeating life patterns that may prevent effective challenging of beliefs

Core beliefs will take some time to change. They have probably been part of your life for a very long time. You may have developed ways of thinking and behaving that make them very hard to shift; ways that make it very difficult to challenge them effectively. Whether or not you are finding it difficult to challenge your core beliefs, challenging them will be made easier by recognising these patterns. Three patterns of thinking and behaviour, or self-defeating life patterns, act to keep them alive. They have been termed surrender, escape and counter-attack.

Surrender

Those who use surrender give in to their core beliefs. They typically distort or misperceive situations in a way that confirms them. They may use selective attention (the thinking bias introduced in Chapter 8), focusing only on situations or events that fit with their poor opinion of themselves. They may distort information that does not support their core beliefs, in an attempt to make it fit. They may reject or not notice evidence that contradicts their beliefs. They think, feel and act in a way that confirms their beliefs. This simply reinforces the power of the beliefs. Gina had the core belief 'I'm inferior'. She put other people's needs before her own, even though she privately felt that others walked all over her. She made a point of putting herself down in front of other people, in the belief that criticising herself wasn't as bad as someone else beating her to it. She also constantly watched out for and noticed any mistakes (however small) that she made. All these strategies served to keep her belief 'I'm inferior' alive.

Escape

Those who use the escape strategy avoid thinking about their negative core beliefs. They also do their utmost to avoid the unpleasant feelings associated with these beliefs. They often avoid situations that might trigger either their negative beliefs or their negative feelings. Bingeing is one powerful way to avoid thinking about negative core beliefs or having the unpleasant feelings that go with them. However, if you use this strategy, the negative core beliefs will remain unchallenged.

Corinne had the core belief 'I'm a failure'. Whenever the slightest thing went wrong (at college or in her relationships) she would turn to bingeing (which she called her 'bulimic bubble') to escape from the real world. More generally, she also avoided difficult situations with people or where she might not do well. All this meant that her belief 'I'm a failure' remained unchallenged.

Counter-attack

The third strategy is counter-attack. Those who use counter-attack try to make up for their negative core beliefs, often by thinking, feeling and behaving in ways that contradict them. This may look like a healthy strategy, particularly when the person seems to feel good about herself. However, underneath, the person feels very vulnerable and the strategy is often pursued in an extreme way, and at the expense of her development and happiness.

Dieting is a form of counter attack; it develops as a way to overcome or make up for negative core beliefs and the unpleasant feelings associated with them. These beliefs are reflected in underlying assumptions where, for example, it is thought that losing weight will help the person feel good about herself and, in addition, that other people will think more of her. However, underneath this facade, the person continues to feel fragile and to think badly about herself. The problem with this strategy is that it is vulnerable to collapse, particularly when dieting is used as a form of counter attack. If dieting fails (or is perceived to fail), as it often does, then the negative core beliefs simply reassert themselves with more determination than ever before.

Angela had the core belief 'I'm a failure'. She dieted to give herself a sense of success and achievement. She also thought her friends would think more of her for having such self-control. However, despite her best intentions she could never keep to her diet. This simply reinforced her feeling of failure and made her feel extremely depressed.

The importance of the past

Core beliefs usually develop in early childhood although in some people with eating disorders they seem to have developed in the teenage years. The three self-defeating life patterns also typically develop at the same time. Negative core beliefs usually develop in response to negative early childhood or teenage experiences. They usually arise from abuse (which may be sexual, physical or emotional), neglect and lack of attention or understanding from parents, teachers or peers.

Maria's parents had very high expectations of her academically and neglected her emotional needs and emotional development. They paid great attention to educational play and to her schoolwork. They criticised her if she failed to achieve A grades and discouraged her from making and spending time with friends. She could not remember being praised for anything other than academic achievement. As a result she formed the beliefs 'I'm a misfit and I'm a failure'. The three self-defeating life patterns develop as ways to cope with these sorts of beliefs. Most people with eating disorders will use all three strategies at one time or another. However, the most common are escape and counter-attack (the use of bingeing to avoid facing beliefs and feelings, and the use of dieting to overcome these).

Reframing the past

People with eating disorders who have suffered at the hands of parents, teachers or peers typically blame themselves for their suffering even though they are rarely to blame. This belief is often firmly held. Even as adults we are usually reluctant to blame those who hurt us as children. Self-blame in bulimia nervosa usually reflects core beliefs and it can be challenged in the same way as other negative core beliefs. It is important to remember that if negative things happened to you in the past it was not your fault. Negative things happen to everyone at some time in their life – would you say that everyone is bad?

When others place too much emphasis on your weight and shape

Sometimes other people attach too much importance to your weight and shape. One problem faced by some women with bulimia nervosa is that they have chosen a partner who places great value on slenderness and attractiveness. Another problem is having chosen a career that requires great attention to weight and shape. Both situations, by encouraging dieting and weight control, may prevent core beliefs and negative thoughts from being challenged and, as a result, make you vulnerable to relapse.

Ros was a dancer in a nightclub. Although she felt accepted by her partner and friends, she had to diet constantly in order to stay slim. She knew her natural weight would be unacceptable to her employer. Sticking with her job thus continually reinforced her belief 'I'm unacceptable'. To overcome her bulimia she had to make a tough decision about her career and her health.

Dealing with difficult relationships

Occasionally women with bulimia nervosa stay in stressful relationships because they feel no one else would accept them, or because they feel they can't do any better. These are complex problems. Once you have overcome your eating disorder you may wish to make changes to such a relationship. Often it can be helpful to seek help from a counsellor. Your GP or family doctor can advise you about this.

Summary exercise

Write a brief summary of what you have learned from this chapter, both from the information presented and from the exercises. Also write down how you will put what you have learned into practice. Then, write the essence of your summary and plans on a small index card. Put this in a bag or inside a diary that you usually carry with you and make time, twice a day, to read the card.

Chapter summary

This chapter has introduced you to several ways to challenge core beliefs. It made the following important points:

- It is important to challenge negative core beliefs, but equally important to build up new, more positive beliefs.

- Core beliefs will usually change relatively slowly; more slowly than thoughts or assumptions.

- Self-defeating life patterns may prevent effective challenging of beliefs. In bulimia nervosa escape (bingeing) and counter-attack (dieting) are particularly important

The following suggestions were made:

- Complete the exercises over a period of weeks or months. Return to them regularly (once a week, if possible) and continue to build on them.

- Challenge your old core beliefs and build new beliefs using the core belief worksheet, cognitive continua, historical tests of beliefs, positive data logs, behavioural experiments and flashcards.

- Identify self-defeating life patterns that may prevent effective challenging of beliefs.

- Reframe the past.

- Tackle any problems that may be making you vulnerable.

CHAPTER 19

Preventing Relapse

You are probably very keen to make sure that your eating problem does not recur. If you have stopped bingeing and engaging in any compensatory behaviours, and you have tackled your underlying assumptions and core beliefs, then this is unlikely. However, it would be unrealistic to think that you will not face some difficult situations in the future. You may well find yourself in situations in which you are tempted to binge, go on a strict diet or return to your old ways of behaving or thinking. In this chapter we will help you develop a blueprint or summary of what you have learned from the programme and, in particular, a summary of what you have found most useful. This will serve as a reminder to you to implement appropriate strategies, if you do feel that you are at risk of relapse or in danger of slipping back into your old ways. We will also suggest other ways in which you can prepare for the future, and prevent relapse.

Exercise to develop a blueprint

To develop a blueprint, complete Worksheet 19.1. Ask yourself all the questions on it. The questions cover the major stages, strategies and techniques that are covered in the programme.

For an example of a completed blueprint look at Hayley's completed worksheet in Box 19.1.

Identifying early warning signs of relapse and developing an action plan

To make sure that you do not relapse it is a good idea to identify what for you might signal that relapse is possible or likely. The sooner you can identify potential problems, the easier it will be to deal with them. Ask yourself what signs would tell you early on that your problems might be returning? Make a list of them in order of their possible appearance, as Philippa did, from very early warning signs to signs that might develop rather later on (see Box 19.2).

Worksheet 19.1 Developing a blueprint

Fears associated with change

How do you feel now about the fears you had at the beginning, before starting to work through the manual? Have the advantages of change outweighed the disadvantages?

Understanding what keeps problem behaviours going; the cognitive model

What different types of thought keep your bingeing going?

Challenging thoughts in the vicious circle

The myth of control

What is the evidence that you do have control (both over eating and over thoughts and feelings)? How have you discovered that this is the case?

Permissive thoughts

What was learned from challenging these thoughts? What questions and strategies were particularly useful?

Positive beliefs about eating

What was learned from challenging these thoughts? What questions and strategies were particularly useful?

Behaviours that keep negative thoughts about weight and shape going

Were fears associated with giving up these behaviours unfounded? What was the effect on negative thoughts of giving up these behaviours?

Underlying assumptions and core beliefs

What was learned about assumptions and core beliefs? What was learned about the role of early experiences?

What was learned from challenging underlying assumptions and core beliefs? What questions and strategies were particularly useful?

Box 19.1 Hayley's completed worksheet: Developing a blueprint

Fears associated with change

I was worried I wouldn't want to give up bingeing and vomiting because I saw it as the only way to eat what I wanted and stay slim. I was also worried that change would mean putting on loads of weight. To my great surprise I now eat all the things I want as part of a normal diet. I have gained a few pounds, though not as much as I feared. This was difficult at first, but now that the rest of my life is so much better I feel all right about it. It's a small price to pay for feeling so much happier.

Understanding what keeps problem behaviours going; the cognitive model

I found that I had lots of positive beliefs about eating. I used to believe that eating would take away all my worries and make me feel better. Once I'd started eating I knew I'd be getting rid of it so I told myself that it was OK to carry on and eat more. I didn't really believe I'd lost control – but I used to say that to myself afterwards to make it feel all right.

Challenging thoughts in the vicious circle

The myth of control

If I'm honest I never really believed deep down inside that I had no control. Binges were always planned and they happened only when I was alone in the evenings and at weekends. I never binged at school or when other people were around.

Permissive thoughts

Once I'd made up my mind to binge I didn't want to challenge my thoughts and it was hard work. The thoughts record was helpful at first but it didn't lead to permanent change. What really helped were the behavioural experiments. I found it useful to write the question 'Am I giving myself permission to binge?' on a flashcard.

Positive beliefs about eating

I believed these for a long time. They seemed a bit trivial at first and it was hard to believe they were important. When I did recognise, from keeping a thoughts record, that they were actually very important. I found writing a flashcard helped me start to challenge them. These questions were particularly useful:

Box 19.1 continued

'If I binge now how will I feel about it at the end of the day?' 'What would be the disadvantages of bingeing?' 'What other ways can I deal with my concerns?'

Behaviours that keep negative thoughts about weight and shape going

I liked the idea of experimenting, before committing myself to permanent change. It was like dipping your toe in the water to test the temperature before diving into the pool. Two experiments were particularly helpful: eating normally for a week, and comparing concentrating on feeling full with distracting myself. I found I didn't gain anywhere near as much weight as I'd predicted, while focusing on feeling full increased my concern about my weight (to my surprise). Challenging my thoughts had helped me to see other options. Dropping some of my problem behaviours made those options permanent, and doing so really did reduce my concerns about my weight, shape and eating.

Underlying assumptions and core beliefs

Assumptions and beliefs are the fuel for thoughts, emotions and behaviour. Because I believed I was a failure, I dieted to try and feel better about myself. However, it was impossible to keep to the very strict diets I went on, and the more I failed at dieting the more I believed I was a complete failure as a person. This meant I tried even harder to diet (so as not to feel a failure). The problem with this was that I thought about little else apart from food and eating. My schoolwork suffered. I lost nearly all my friends and I couldn't think straight. My early experiences, especially being constantly compared to my very clever sister, probably had a role in making me feel a failure. Challenging my core beliefs made me realise I'm not a complete failure. I've failed at a few things (like most people) but I'm also good at quite a lot of things. I found the positive data log very helpful in collecting evidence for my new core belief 'I'm successful at quite a few things'. I also realised that it's not helpful to blame people for what happened in the past. What matters is how I interpreted what happened to me and how I (and others) have unwittingly gone on reinforcing that over the years.

Box 19.2 Philippa's early warning signs

- Looking in the mirror more frequently.

- Checking my shape.

- Feeling more aware of what my clothes look like.

- Thinking about calorie values.

- Thinking about restricting my food.

- Serious dieting.

Next, try to identify what action you can take, as soon as they are noticed, to prevent yourself from relapsing. This may involve reading through your blueprint and returning to some of the strategies and techniques that you found helpful earlier in the programme. If they are not already on your blueprint list the specific techniques and strategies that you found most helpful and that you could use again. Philippa's plan to deal with her early warning signs can be seen in Box 19.3.

Box 19.3 Philippa's plan to deal with her early warning signs

- Understand my concern using the cognitive model.

- Remind myself of the link between behaviours and negative thoughts about my weight and shape.

- Make plans to drop problem behaviours - repeat behavioural experiments to test out fears if necessary.

- Ask myself 'what are the consequences of losing weight?'

- Refer to my flashcard 'pros and cons of losing weight'.

- Go over my assumption worksheets to remind myself that my self-worth doesn't depend on my weight.

- Make sure I am continuing to work on building up my new core beliefs.

Difficulties and problems over the next few months and strategies for dealing with these

Eating disorders can recur in response to stress. Think ahead over the next few months and ask yourself what problems and difficulties you might have to manage. These could be exams, a house move, going to stay with your parents, the anniversary of a death, the birth of a new baby, leaving school, starting college, having to look for a job, or a child starting school. Make a list of them and then ask yourself how these might be tackled. List specific techniques and strategies that you can use, drawing on what you have learned in the course of the programme.

Identifying lifestyle changes and developing plans for carrying these out

You may have decided that you need to make some changes to your lifestyle. Think carefully about the difficulties that you might have in introducing them and, as before, make a list of how they might be tackled. Make sure you list specific techniques and strategies, drawing on what you have learned in the programme.

Identifying remaining problems and developing plans for change

Finally, you may have identified some other more general problems in the course of working through the programme and overcoming your eating disorder. You may wish to do some further work on these problems. Make a list of them and decide on some specific techniques and strategies to tackle each one. This may involve further reading and further self-help. Look in Appendix 4 for books that use cognitive therapy strategies to tackle problems that may remain.

Summary exercise

Write a brief summary of what you have learned from this chapter, both from the information presented and from the exercises. Also write down how you will put what you have learned into practice. Then, write the essence of your summary and plans on a small index card. Put this in a bag or inside a diary that you usually carry with you and make time, twice a day, to read the card.

Chapter summary

In this chapter we have helped you reduce the possibility of relapse and prepare for the future. The following important points were made:

- It would be unrealistic to think that you will not face some difficult situations in the future.

- You can prepare yourself for these by looking ahead, reminding yourself of what you have learned and what has been most helpful, and by making plans to return to helpful strategies at times of difficulty.

- You may also wish to consider more general lifestyle changes.

The following suggestions were made:

- Develop a blueprint or summary of what you have learned and what has been most useful.

- Identify early warning signs that may signal relapse and develop an action plan to deal with them.

- Identify any problems and difficulties that you may face over the next few months and make a plan to deal with them.

- Identify any lifestyle changes that you wish to make and make a plan to implement these changes.

- Finally, consider whether you wish to make any other more general changes; if so, plan how you will do this.

Further reading

We have included a brief selection of books that you might want to consult for help with any remaining difficulties you may have (Appendix 4). We have also included a selection of books that therapists might find useful.

Final words

We hope that you have found the book and self-help programme helpful. If you have overcome your bulimia nervosa, then that's marvellous and we wish you all the best for the future. If you have made progress, but still feel that you have some way to go, then that's also good news. It suggests that this sort of approach can help you. However, you may want to think about consulting your GP or family doctor for advice. It may be that referral for individual cognitive therapy could help you make further progress. Finally, it may be that you like the approach we have taken but have found it impossible to make headway on your own. Don't despair – consult your GP or family doctor and ask to be referred for individual cognitive therapy. Remember, if you are referred to a cognitive therapist for individual help you may well be able to use or continue to use the programme.

Working out your
body mass index (BMI)

If you are more familiar with pounds and inches use Method 1. If you are more familiar with kilograms and metres use Method 2. In both cases you will need a calculator.

Method 1: Pounds and inches

Step 1: Multiply your weight (in pounds) by 700.

Step 2: Divide the result by your height (in inches).

Step 3: Divide the result by your height (in inches) a second time. This is your BMI.

Example:

For someone whose weight is 130 lbs and whose height is 64":

Step 1: $130 \times 700 = 91,000$

Step 2: $91,000 \div 64 = 1,422$

Step 3: $1,422 \div 64 = 22.2$

BMI is therefore 22.2.

Method 2: Kilograms and metres

Step 1: Multiply your height (in metres) by your height (in metres).

Step 2: Divide your weight (in kilograms) by your answer to Step 1. This is your BMI.

Example:

For someone whose weight is 70 kg and whose height is 1.68 m:

Step 1: $1.68 \times 1.68 = 2.82$

Step 2: $70 \div 2.82 = 23$

BMI is therefore 24.8.

Blank copies of worksheets

Worksheet 5.1 Problems and Goals	
Problems	**Goals**

Worksheet 6.1 Advantages of changing, fears and responses to fears

Advantages	Fears	Responses to fears

Outcome:

Worksheet 6.2 Examining specific (personal and sensitive) fears

What you predict will happen:

How likely is it that this will happen (0–100%)?

Evidence for:	Evidence against:

Outcome: How likely do you think it is now that this will happen (0–100%)?

Conclusion:

Worksheet 7.1 An A-B-C analysis

As or activating events	Bs or thoughts	Cs or consequences

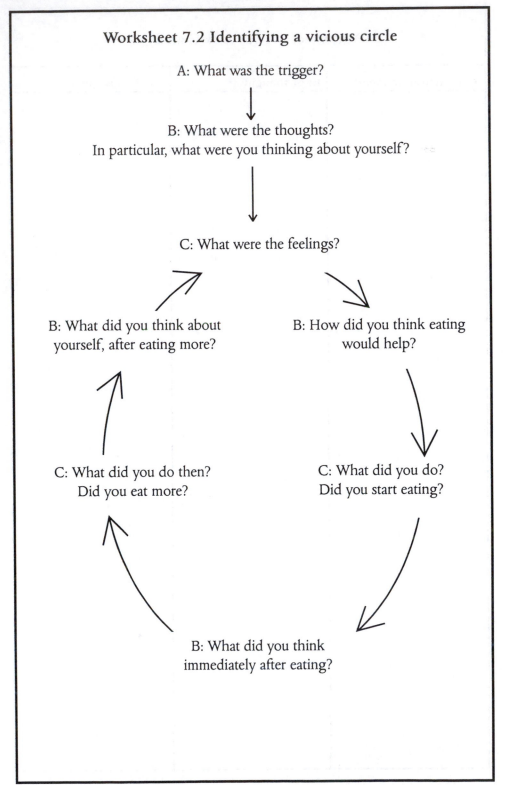

Worksheet 7.2 Identifying a vicious circle

A: What was the trigger?

B: What were the thoughts?
In particular, what were you thinking about yourself?

C: What were the feelings?

B: What did you think about
yourself, after eating more?

B: How did you think eating
would help?

C: What did you do then?
Did you eat more?

C: What did you do?
Did you start eating?

B: What did you think
immediately after eating?

Worksheet 8.1 Evidence for and against
lack of control over eating

Lack of control thoughts:	Belief in each (0–100%):

Evidence for	Evidence against

Outcome:

Re-rate belief in each thought (0–100%):

Worksheet 9.1 Hierarchy of difficult situations

Situation	Difficulty (0–100%)	Order

Worksheet 9.2 Recording behavioural experiments to test thoughts of no control

Thought to be tested:

Belief that the thought is true (0–100%):

Experiment to test thought	Likely problems	Strategies to deal with problems	Date of experiment	Outcome of experiment	Belief in thought (0–100%)

Worksheet 10.1 Identifying permissive thoughts using a thoughts record

Situation	Feelings and sensations	Permissive thoughts
• When was it? • Where were you? • Who were you with? • What were you doing? • What were you thinking about?	• What feelings did you have? • What body sensations did you notice?	• What were you saying to yourself that made it easier to keep eating? • Identify and circle the hot thought. This is the thought that makes it most likely that you will binge.

Worksheet 11.1 Thoughts record for challenging permissive thoughts about eating

Situation	Feelings and sensations	Permissive thoughts	Evidence that does not support the hot thought	Alternative, more helpful thought	Belief in alternative thought
• When was it? • Where were you? • Who were you with? • What were you doing? • What were you thinking about?	• How were you feeling? • What body sensations did you notice?	• What were you saying that made it easier to keep eating? • Identify and circle the hot thought. This is the thought that makes it most likely that you will keep eating and go on to binge.	• Use the questions in Boxes 11.1 and 11.2 to challenge your hot thought.	• Write down an alternative, more helpful thought.	• Rate how much you believe this thought to be true on a scale from 0 to 100%.

Worksheet 12.1 Identifying positive beliefs about eating using a thoughts record

Situation	Feelings and sensations	Positive beliefs about eating
• When was it? • Where were you? • Who were you with? • What were you doing? • What were you thinking about?	• How did you feel? • What body sensations did you notice?	• How did you think eating would help? • What were you afraid might happen if you didn't eat? • Identify and circle the hot thought. This is the thought that makes it most likely that you will eat/binge.

Worksheet 13.1 Thoughts record for challenging positive beliefs about eating

Situation	Feelings and sensations	Positive thoughts about eating	Evidence that does not support the hot thought	Alternative, more helpful thought	Belief in alternative thought
• When was it? • Where were you? • Who were you with? • What were you doing? • What were you thinking about?	• How did you feel? • What body sensations did you notice?	• What were you saying that made it easier to start eating? • Identify and circle the hot thought. This is the thought that makes it most likely that you will start eating and go on to binge.	• Use the questions in Boxes 13.1 and 13.2 to challenge your hot thought.	• Write down an alternative, more helpful thought.	• Rate how much you believe this Thought to be true on a scale from 0 to 100%

Worksheet 14.1 Recording scores on the Behaviours Questionnaire

Subscale	Score
Dieting	
Weight and shape	
Food	

Worksheet 14.2 Fears about giving up the behaviours that maintain negative thoughts

Dieting behaviour
Fear:

Weight and shape related behaviour
Fear:

Food related behaviour
Fear:

Worksheet 14.3 Planning and recording behavioural experiments to test fears about giving up behaviours

Thought to be tested:

Belief that the thought is true (0–100%):

Experiment to test thought	Likely problems	Strategies to deal with problems	Date of experiment	Outcome of experiment	Belief in thought (0–100%)

Worksheet 15.1 Using the downward arrow technique to identify assumptions

Step 1: Setting the scene

- When was the last time that you felt really worried, anxious or bad about your eating (not a binge episode)?

- Imagine that situation.

- What do you see, hear, feel (on your skin), smell?

- What were the triggers?

- How do you feel?

- What thoughts do you have?

- What images/pictures do you have?

- What thoughts do you have in the images?

Worksheet 15.1 Using the downward arrow technique to identify assumptions (continued)

Step 2: Identify the most distressing thought

Which is the most distressing thought?

Step 3: Downward arrow questions

To identify assumptions related to self-acceptance:

• What would that mean about you or say about you?

• What's the worst that it could mean or say about you?

The assumption I hold is:

To identify assumptions related to acceptance by others:

• What do you think other people would think about you or do to you?

• What's the worst that they could think or do?

The assumption I hold is:

Worksheet 16.1 Examining the advantages and disadvantages of assumptions

The assumption I hold is:

Belief in the assumption (0–100%):

Advantages	Disadvantages

Outcome:

Belief in the assumption now (0–100%):

Worksheet 16.2 Examining the evidence for and against and disadvantages of assumptions

The assumption I hold is:

Belief in the assumption (0–100%):	

Evidence against:

Advantages	Disadvantages

Outcome:

Belief in the assumption now (0–100%):

Worksheet 16.3 Identifying the origins of an assumption

The assumption I hold is:

Belief in the assumption (0–100%):

Where did the assumption come from?

When did I first find myself thinking like this?

What was going on in my life at that time?

Conclusion:

Belief in the assumption now (0–100%):

Worksheet 16.4 Planning and recording behavioural experiments to test assumptions

The assumption I hold is:

Belief that the assumption is true (0–100%):

Experiment to test assumption	Likely problems	Strategies to deal with problems	Date of experiment	Outcome of experiment	Belief in thought (0–100%)

Worksheet 17.1 The sentence completion task

I am ....

I am ....

I am ....

Worksheet 17.2 Using the downward arrow technique to identify core beliefs

To identify negative self-beliefs

Summarise assumptions about yourself:

Ask:

- What would that mean about you or say about you?

- What's the worst that it could mean or say about you?

Summarise negative self-beliefs:

Finally ask: Do the core beliefs you have identified reflect your general beliefs about yourself?

Worksheet 17.3 Identifying the relationship between bingeing, dieting and negative self-beliefs

When you feel distressed and think I'm (summarise your negative self-beliefs) is there anything you could do or actually do to change how you feel or think?

Worksheet 18.1 Core belief worksheet

Old core belief:

Belief in it now (0–100%):

New core belief:

Belief in it now (0–100%):

Evidence that contradicts old core belief and supports new belief	Evidence that supports old core belief with reframe

Old core belief:	**New core belief:**
Belief in it now (0–100%):	**Belief in it now (0–100%):**

Worksheet 18.2 Cognitive continua

| 0 | 10 | 20 | 30 | 40 | 50 | 60 | 70 | 80 | 90 | 100 |

Old belief   **New belief**

| 0 | 10 | 20 | 30 | 40 | 50 | 60 | 70 | 80 | 90 | 100 |

| 0 | 10 | 20 | 30 | 40 | 50 | 60 | 70 | 80 | 90 | 100 |

| 0 | 10 | 20 | 30 | 40 | 50 | 60 | 70 | 80 | 90 | 100 |

| 0 | 10 | 20 | 30 | 40 | 50 | 60 | 70 | 80 | 90 | 100 |

| 0 | 10 | 20 | 30 | 40 | 50 | 60 | 70 | 80 | 90 | 100 |

etc.

Worksheet 18.3 Historical test of beliefs

Old core belief:

New core belief:

Prediction if I look over my lifetime:

Age	Experiences I had that are consistent with the old core belief with reframe	Experiences I had that are consistent with the new core belief
0–2		
Summary:		
3–5		
Summary:		
6–12		
Summary:		
13–18		
Summary:		

Worksheet 18.3 Historical test of beliefs (continued)

Age	Experiences I had that are consistent with the old core belief with reframe	Experiences I had that are consistent with the new core belief
19–25		
Summary:		
26–35		
Summary:		
36+		
Summary:		

Overall summary:

Compare outcome of historical test of core belief to prediction:

Re-rate old and new core beliefs:

Old core belief (0–100%):

New core belief (0–100%):

Worksheet 18.4 Planning and recording behavioural experiments to test predictions based on core beliefs

Core belief to be tested:

Belief that the core belief is true (0–100%):

Experiment to test core belief	Likely problems	Strategies to deal with problems	Date of experiment	Outcome of experiment	Belief in core belief (0–100%)

Worksheet 19.1 Developing a blueprint

Fears associated with change

How do you feel now about the fears you had at the beginning, before starting to work through the manual? Have the advantages of change outweighed the disadvantages?

Understanding what keeps problem behaviours going; the cognitive model

What different types of thought keep your bingeing going?

Challenging thoughts in the vicious circle

The myth of control

What is the evidence that you do have control (both over eating and over thoughts and feelings)? How have you discovered that this is the case?

Permissive thoughts

What was learned from challenging these thoughts? What questions and strategies were particularly useful?

Worksheet 19.1 Developing a blueprint (continued)

Positive beliefs about eating
What was learned from challenging these thoughts? What questions and strategies were particularly useful?

Behaviours that keep negative thoughts about weight and shape going

Were fears associated with giving up these behaviours unfounded? What was the effect on negative thoughts of giving up these behaviours?

Underlying assumptions and core beliefs

What was learned about assumptions and core beliefs? What was learned about the role of early experiences?

What was learned from challenging underlying assumptions and core beliefs? What questions and strategies were particularly useful?

APPENDIX 3

Distinguishing between Thoughts and Feelings

Exercise

Completing this exercise will help you to distinguish more clearly between thoughts and feelings. Use Worksheet A1 and follow the steps below.

Worksheet A1 Identifying thoughts and feelings	
I'm fat	Thought
I'm frightened	Feeling
I'm going to gain weight	Thought
I've lost control	
No one cares about me	
I'm sad	
I'm anxious	
I'm a blob	
I'm frightened	
No one likes me	
I'm miserable	
I'm worried	
I'm a failure	
I won't get better	
I'm stupid	
She thinks I'm no good	
I feel tearful	
I'm panicky	

Step 1

Read each statement in the left-hand column and next to it in the right-hand column write whether this is a thought or a feeling. The first three are done for you.

Step 2

Look at the answers in Box A1 and check them against your answers.

Step 3

If you had difficulty with this read 'a note about thoughts and feelings' in Chapter 7 again.

Box A1 Thoughts – feelings answers

I'm fat	Thought
I'm frightened	Feeling
I'm going to gain weight	Thought
I've lost control	Thought
No one cares about me	Thought
I'm sad	Feeling
I'm anxious	Feeling
I'm a blob	Thought
I'm frightened	Feeling
No one likes me	Thought
I'm miserable	Feeling
I'm worried	Feeling
I'm a failure	Thought
I won't get better	Thought
I'm stupid	Thought
She thinks I'm no good	Thought
I feel tearful	Feeling
I'm panicky	Feeling

APPENDIX 4

Additional Reading

All the books suggested are self-help books, and all draw on cognitive therapy strategies.

Burns, D.D. (1980) *Feeling Good: The New Mood Therapy*. New York: Signet.
One of the first self-help cognitive therapy books, which focuses particularly on overcoming depression and hopelessness.

Burns, D.D. (1989) *The Feeling Good Handbook*. New York: Plume.
This book suggests strategies for dealing with depression, anxiety, fears and phobias, low self-esteem and relationship difficulties.

Butler, G. and Hope, T. (1995) *Manage your Mind*. Oxford: Oxford University Press.
A general guide, dealing with a wide range of issues, from anxiety and depression to effective study. The chapter on good eating habits is likely to be particularly useful if you have an eating disorder.

Fennell, M.J.V. (1999) *Overcoming Low Self-esteem*. London: Robinson Publishing.
This book is particularly useful if you have persistent, long standing low self-esteem.

Greenberger, D. and Padesky, C.A. (1995) *Mind Over Mood: A Cognitive Therapy Treatment Manual for Clients*. New York: Guilford Press.
This book introduces the basics of cognitive therapy. It is particularly helpful in understanding and changing depression, anxiety, anger, guilt and shame.

Reading for therapists

Beck, A.T., Rush, A.J., Shaw, B.F. and Emery, G. (1979) *Cognitive Therapy of Depression*. New York: Guilford Press.

Beck, A.T., Emery, G. and Greenberg, R.L. (1985) *Anxiety Disorders and Phobias: A Cognitive Perspective*. New York: Guilford Press.

Padesky, C.A. and Greenberger, D. (1995) *Clinician's Guide to Mind over Mood*. New York: Guilford Press.

Useful Addresses: Eating Disorder Organisations

The addresses below are good starting points for seeking out local self-help organisations, and local sources of information.

Argentina
Association Against Bulimia and Anorexia
Av. Pueryrredon 1775(1119)
Buenos Aires, Argentina

Australia
Anorexia and Bulimia Nervosa Foundation
1513 High Street
Glen Iris VIC 3146, Australia

Canada
National Eating Disorder Information Centre
CW1-304, 200 Elizabeth Street
Toronto
Ontario M5G 2C4, Canada

Denmark
Spiseroet
Mejlgade eetude 49
Aarhus 8000, Denmark

France
Groupe d'étude français de l'anorexie et boulimie
Maison de l'home
54 Boulevard Rapail
Paris 75006, France

Japan
Yokohama
Women's Association for Communication and Networking
Landmark Tower, 13th Floor
1-2-1-1 Minato-Mirai
Nishi-Ku
Yokohama 220-8113, Japan

Netherlands

Stichting Anorexia & Boulimia Nervosa
PO Box 67
NL 6880 AB
Velp, The Netherlands

New Zealand

Eating Disorders Association (NZ)
Inc. PO Box 80–142
Green Bay
Auckland, New Zealand

Norway

Anorexia/Bulimia
Foreningen Postboks 36
Bergen 5001, Norway

Spain

Adaner
C/General Pardinas 3-1 O A
Madrid 28001, Spain

Sweden

Anorexia/Bulimia Kontact
Regenringsgantan 88
11139 Stockholm, Sweden

Switzerland

Association Boulimie et Anorexie
Avenue de Villamont
Lausanne CH 1005, Switzerland

UK

Eating Disorders Association
First Floor, Wensum House
103 Prince of Wales Road
Norwich NR1 1DW, UK

USA

American Anorexia/Bulimia Association Inc.
418 East 76th Street
New York 10021, USA

A Cognitive Model of Bulimia Nervosa:

Theory and Evidence

This appendix will provide an overview of recent developments in cognitive theory, together with a brief summary of early cognitive models of bulimia nervosa. It will then introduce the cognitive theory on which the programme outlined in this book is based. A brief review of the evidence that supports this theory will be conducted, together with a summary of how existing evidence is consistent with its' main features. Finally, its consistency with recent developments in theories of normal eating will be evaluated.

Cognitive models

Cognitive models of psychiatric disorders were first developed by Beck, initially for depression (Beck, Rush, Shaw and Emery 1979), later for anxiety disorders (Beck, Emery and Greenberg 1985) and, more recently, for personality disorders (Beck and Freeman 1990). Their key assumption is that emotional distress (and problematic behaviour) is maintained by the interpretation of events (internal and external) rather than by the events themselves. Thoughts and beliefs thus play an extremely important role in treatment. By modifying them, feelings and behaviours can be changed.

Cognitive models have two parts to them: features that explain the maintenance of a disorder and features that explain its development. In early texts the models were relatively uncomplicated and often generic in application, this was particularly true of developmental explanations. More recently, detailed vicious circles have been developed to explain the maintenance of specific disorders, particularly anxiety disorders (Wells 1997). At the same time, there has been increased interest in the development of disorders, and a more detailed generic developmental cognitive model has been outlined (J.S. Beck, 1995). Nowadays, maintenance models involve a series of vicious circles. These usually include thoughts, feelings, behaviour (and, in some cases, physiology). Developmental models involve an implied causal sequence. This usually involves beliefs and assumptions, both of which may be shaped by certain early experiences. Beliefs and assumptions can lie dormant until triggered by a relevant critical event; the combination with the critical event triggers off the vicious circles that produce the active disorder. Maintenance models are often associated with acute, relatively circumscribed problems, while developmental models are often associated with chronic, long-standing problems. In eating disorders, both tend to be present, thus models of bulimia nervosa typically need to incorporate both elements.

Cognitive models of bulimia nervosa

Early cognitive models of bulimia nervosa (Fairburn, Cooper and Cooper 1986) were based on Garner and Bemis's (1982) cognitive model of anorexia nervosa. This in turn was based on Beck's model of depression (Beck *et al.* 1979). They also drew on the ideas of restraint theory. This suggested that some people 'restrained eaters', attempt to maintain their body weight below its set point and are thus chronically hungry and prone to overeat in response to external cues (Herman and Mack 1975). The cognitive model emphasised the role of automatic thoughts, underlying assumptions and information processing (which could be reflected in both automatic thoughts and underlying assumptions). Restraint theory emphasised the role of dieting, as well as a deficit model of eating, with hunger and satiety largely determined by physiological mechanisms. Putting the two together created a model in which underlying assumptions reflected overvalued ideas about dieting and weight loss (as a long-term strategy). Dieting, in the context of set point theory, also meant that chronic hunger was present; thus making overeating more likely, particularly in the short term. Overeating was also facilitated by cognitions, particularly dichotomous thinking, as well as maintained (according to restraint theory) by impaired satiety mechanisms. Additionally, binge eating and vomiting maintained low self-esteem; while vomiting encouraged binge eating. The model was conceived of primarily as a model of maintenance; it did not attempt to explain the development of the disorder. One of the major goals of treatment, in addition to addressing cognitive distortions about weight and shape, was eating three meals a day plus snacks and the elimination of dieting.

A new cognitive model of bulimia nervosa

Building on recent developments in cognitive theory and on our research findings, we have devised a new cognitive model of bulimia nervosa. It explains the maintenance of binge eating, incorporating several types of thoughts, feelings and behaviour, as well as physiological processes, in vicious circles. It also explains the development of the disorder in some detail, drawing on the concepts of underlying assumptions, core beliefs and schema driven processes.

A model of maintenance

In the model a trigger activates a negative self-belief. This gives rise to negative automatic thoughts and to negative feelings, creating a route into a vicious circle. Thoughts in the vicious circle include beliefs about how eating will help with the negative thoughts and feelings; beliefs about the negative consequences of eating; permissive thoughts and thoughts of no control. These act to encourage eating and, as the vicious circle revolves, bingeing. More specifically, positive beliefs about eating (how eating will help) act together with negative beliefs (the negative consequences of eating), creating cognitive dissonance, and as a result emotional distress. This is resolved by permissive thoughts, including thoughts of no control. Once eating takes place the vicious circle links back to negative self-beliefs, revolving again and again until a binge occurs.

A model of development

In the developmental model, negative early experiences give rise to dysfunctional beliefs, particularly negative self-beliefs (one type of core belief). These are absolute, unconditional beliefs about the self. Schema compensation strategies develop to cope with or manage these beliefs. The most common strategy that develops in bulimia nervosa is dieting; and this is reflected in the content of underlying assumptions. In bulimia nervosa three types of underlying assumption seem to be important, two related to weight and shape and one related to eating. The weight and shape assumptions concern these attributes as a means to self-acceptance and as a means to acceptance by other people. Eating related assumptions can also concern self (more common) acceptance or acceptance by other people. Major goals of treatment are to address cognitions in the vicious circle that maintain binge-eating, together with the assumptions and beliefs that explain the development of the disorder.

Evidence for the new model

We have conducted a series of studies that provide evidence for our model.

A semi-structured interview

This study (Cooper, Todd and Wells 1998) provided information relevant to maintenance processes and developmental factors.

MAINTENANCE PROCESSES

We found that initial triggers for binge eating included situations unrelated to weight, shape and eating, as well as situations related to these. Focus on bodily sensations could also trigger a binge. Bingeing then provided short-term relief from the associated negative thoughts and feelings. Four types of thought seemed to be important and completed a vicious circle:

- positive beliefs about eating;
- negative beliefs about weight and shape;
- permissive thoughts;
- thoughts of no control.

Negative self-beliefs (core beliefs about the self) were also important.

DEVELOPMENTAL FACTORS

Three types of belief were identified. These were negative self-beliefs and two types of underlying assumptions: weight and shape as a means to self-acceptance, and weight and shape as a means to acceptance by others. Both positive and negative underlying assumptions (of both types) were identified. These assumptions reflected schema compensation beliefs (Young 1990) and provided a mechanism linking core beliefs to dieting behaviour. We found that certain early experiences appeared to have a role in the development of both negative self-beliefs and the two types of underlying assumptions. We also identified two types of eating related assumptions. First order assumptions linked eating behaviour with weight gain; second order assumptions linked eating behaviour with core beliefs. Both positive and negative assumptions could be identified.

The eating disorder belief questionnaire

We developed this measure, a self-report questionnaire, to assess negative self-beliefs and underlying assumptions about weight and shape (Cooper, Cohen-Tovée, Todd, Wells and Tovée 1997). Factor analysis confirmed the reliability and validity of negative self-beliefs and the two types of assumption about weight and shape. In addition, multiple regression analyses indicated that negative self-beliefs seemed to be generic beliefs, associated with general distress, while the assumptions were specifically related to eating disorder symptoms. Consistent with this finding a further study has indicated that while depressed patients and patients with bulimia nervosa do not differ in negative self-beliefs, the bulimia nervosa patients score significantly more highly on the assumption sub-scales (Cooper and Hunt 1998). A related study (with anorexia nervosa patients, rather than bulimics) found that normal dieters differed from controls on all subscales of the measure (Cooper and Turner 2000), suggesting that the beliefs and assumptions we have identified are not also characteristic of normal dieters.

Sentence completion

A small study, using a sentence completion task (Padesky and Mooney 1995) confirmed that negative self-beliefs are important in bulimia nervosa (Cooper, Todd and Cohen-Tovee 1996). It also suggested that negative self-beliefs may be relatively more important than beliefs about others and beliefs about the world.

Consistency with existing empirical findings

Early experiences

There are many reports of early childhood trauma or early negative experiences in bulimia nervosa (Guidano and Liotti 1983). This may include childhood sexual abuse, found in a wide range of psychiatric disorders, not just bulimia nervosa, (Welch and Fairburn 1994); physical and emotional abuse (Rorty, Yager and Rossotto 1994); or simple neglect, indifference or lack of attention. Such experiences typically result in the development of the types of negative self-beliefs we have identified as being important in bulimia nervosa.

Low self-esteem

Included in our model, in the form of negative self-beliefs, low self-esteem has long been assumed to be a key feature of bulimia nervosa. Although not often investigated systematically, several studies indicate that patients with bulimia nervosa have low self-esteem (e.g. Jones, Peveler, Hope and Fairburn 1993), often as low as that observed in depressed patients.

Self-worth linked to weight and shape

Our model is consistent with clinical, empirical and theoretical ideas that suggest a link between self-worth and weight and shape (reflected in our model as a schema compensation strategy). Clinically, the link has been frequently observed between dieting in bulimia nervosa and the importance of judging self-worth in terms of weight and shape (Fairburn and Cooper 1989). In particular, it has been observed that weight and shape concerns are related to feelings of worthlessness and ineffectiveness. A positive association between thinness and happiness and success has also been noted (Lacey 1984). Empirically, the link has been investigated with the Shape and Weight Based Self-Esteem Inventory (Geller, Johnston and Madston 1997). Although the items are not expressed in cognitive terms, the findings it has produced are consistent with the links we suggest. Relevant to theory a review, designed to provide a framework for research into cognitive aspects of eating disorders (Vitousek and Hollon 1990), also highlights a cognitive link (through the concept weight related self-schemata) between weight and shape and self-worth.

Dieting

Although not a requirement for a DSM-IV diagnosis (American Psychiatric Association, 1994) extreme dieting is also a feature of bulimia nervosa. Many studies, using well-validated measures indicate that patients with bulimia nervosa often diet or severely restrict their food intake (Fairburn and Cooper 1984). This is reflected in our theory in underlying assumptions.

Bingeing

TRIGGERS FOR BINGEING

Many studies have shown that binge-eating in bulimia nervosa is preceded by considerable distress; both emotionally and cognitively (e.g. Abraham and Beumont 1982, for cognitions; Elmore and De Castro 1990, for emotions). This is consistent with our model.

DISTRACTION FROM THOUGHTS AND FEELINGS

Several studies indicate that bingeing gives relief from distress, particularly anxiety (Kaye, Gwirtsman, George, Weiss and Jimerson 1986) but also depression (Hsu 1990). Again, this is consistent with our model, particularly with the concept positive beliefs about eating.

CONCERN ABOUT WEIGHT AND SHAPE

Fear of weight gain is a defining feature of bulimia nervosa, and a criteria for making a DSM-IV diagnosis (American Psychiatric Association, 1994). It is a pervasive fear, preceding as well as following bingeing (Fairburn 1986). This fits with our concept of negative beliefs about weight and shape.

Permissive thoughts

These have been widely assessed using self-report inventories (Cooper and Fairburn 1992; Phelan 1987). They include dichotomous thinking, first identified by Fairburn as typical of the negative self-statements characteristic of bulimia nervosa (Fairburn et al. 1986). In all studies patients with bulimia nervosa endorse such cognitions very strongly. Our theory includes these thoughts.

Control thoughts

Belief in lack of control over eating during a binge is also a defining feature, and necessary for a diagnosis of bulimia nervosa (American Psychiatric Association 1994). Self-report measures have been used to assess these, including widely used measures (e.g. the Eating Attitudes Test, Garner and Garfinkel 1979), and measures designed for specific studies (e.g. Cooper and Fairburn 1992). Bulimia nervosa patients typically endorse such cognitions very strongly. They are included in our model.

Consequences of bingeing

Immediately after bingeing and before purging negative emotions increase, particularly depression (Elmore and De Castro 1990; Hsu 1990). Negative cognitions focused on self-loathing also intensify, especially guilt and disgust (Cooper, Morrison, Bigman, Abramowitz, Levin and Krener 1988). This is consistent with our suggestion that eating, as the vicious circle revolves, links back to negative self-beliefs.

Theories of normal eating

Restraint theory

Restraint theory has recently been questioned as a paradigm for bulimia nervosa (Lowe, Gleaves, DiSimone-Weiss, Furgueson, Gayda, Kolsky, Neal-Walden, Nelson and McKinney 1996). For example, it has been found that restrained eating and current dieting, although associated with more symptoms related to bulimia, are not associated with binge eating itself. It has been suggested (Lowe, Gleaves and Murphy-Eberenz 1998), and there is some evidence, that although weight loss dieting plays a role in its development, it may be less important in the maintenance of binge eating than was once thought (Lowe et al. 1996). Other research groups are producing findings consistent with this suggestion (e.g. Steiger, Lehoux and Gauvin 1999; Stice and Agras 1998; Stice, Nemeroff and Shaw 1996). The findings have implications for treatment based on cognitive models. In particular, they suggest that the elimination of dieting may not be such an important strategy in the reduction of binge-eating as had been initially thought. They do, however, suggest that dieting may play a role in its development.

'Set point' assumptions

The assumptions on which restraint theory rests have also been questioned, as theories of normal eating have developed. In particular, its two 'set point' assumptions have been criticised. The first, that body weight is regulated (i.e. eating can be affected by deviations from a hypothetical body fat set point). The second, that meal initiation and termination is regulated (i.e. eating is affected by deviations from a hypothetical blood glucose set point). The two assumptions are complementary and, in early cognitive theories, the former provides the context for the latter.

Criticisms of set point

Recently it has been argued that set point theories have serious weaknesses (Pinel 2000). In particular, they are unable to account for all the evidence. As explanations for meal initiation and termination they have begun to be replaced by alternative theories. These suggest that we are drawn to eat not by an internal energy deficit but by the anticipated pleasure of eating. Moreover, in such theories (known as positive incentive theories), hunger felt at any one time depends on an interaction between internal influences, i.e. gastrointestinal and metabolic, and dietary and external influences, all of which can be influenced by learning. Set point theory of body weight regulation is also unable to explain all the research findings. Recently, it has been replaced by the concept of a 'settling point'. This is defined as a 'point at which various factors that influence the level of some regulated function achieve an equilibrium', Pinel 2000, p.267. It provides a loose homeostatic mechanism without the assumption of a set point. It is more consistent with recent data and, where it makes the same prediction as set point, it is more parsimonious.

Theories of normal eating and our model

Positive incentive theories are consistent with our model, in which positive beliefs about eating play an important role in initiating binge-eating. The available evidence on the role of psychological factors in meal initiation and termination (Pinel 2000) is also consistent with it. Findings using the Eating Expectancy Inventory also provide some preliminary evidence that positive expectancies about eating are related to bulimic symptoms (Hohlstein, Smith and Atlas 1998).

Our theory is also consistent with settling theories, in that it does not assume that body weight is regulated around a set point.

Summary

We have presented a new model of bulimia nervosa. The model is consistent with recent developments in cognitive models. It is backed by empirical research designed to test it and is consistent with major existing empirical findings. It is also consistent with recent findings on the role of dieting in bulimia nervosa and with recent developments in theories of normal eating.

References

Abraham, S.F. and Beumont, P.J.V. (1982) 'How patients describe bulimia or binge eating.' *Psychological Medicine 12*, 625–635.

American Psychiatric Association (1994) *DSM-IV*. Washington, DC: American Psychiatric Association.

Beck, A.T. and Freeman, A. (1990) *Cognitive Therapy of Personality Disorders*. New York: Guilford Press.

Beck, A.T., Emery, G. and Greenberg, R.L. (1985) *Anxiety Disorders and Phobias: A Cognitive Perspective*. New York: Guilford Press.

Beck, A.T., Rush, A.J., Shaw, B.F. and Emery, G. (1979) *Cognitive Therapy of Depression*. New York: Guilford Press.

Cooper, J.L., Morrison, T.L., Bigman, O.L., Abramowitz, S.I., Levin, S. and Krener, P. (1988) 'Mood changes and affective disorder in the bulimic binge–purge cycle.' *International Journal of Eating Disorders 7*, 469–474.

Cooper, M.J., Cohen-Tovée, E., Todd, G., Wells, A. and Tovée, M. (1997) 'A questionnaire to assess assumptions and beliefs in eating disorders: Preliminary findings.' *Behaviour Research and Therapy 35*, 381–388.

Cooper, M.J. and Fairburn, C.G. (1992) 'Thoughts about eating, weight and shape in anorexia nervosa and bulimia nervosa.' *Behaviour Research and Therapy 30*, 501–511.

Cooper, M.J. and Hunt, J. (1998) 'Core beliefs and underlying assumptions in bulimia nervosa and depression.' *Behaviour Research and Therapy 36*, 895–898.

Cooper, M.J. and Turner, H. (2000) 'Underlying assumptions and core beliefs in anorexia nervosa and dieting.' *British Journal of Psychotherapy, 39*, 215–218.

Cooper, M.J., Todd, G. and Cohen-Tovée, E. (1996) 'Core beliefs in eating disorders.' *International Cognitive Therapy Newsletter 10*, 2, 2–3.

Cooper, M.J., Todd, G. and Wells, A. (1998) 'Content, origins, and consequences of dysfunctional beliefs in anorexia nervosa and bulimia nervosa.' *Journal of Cognitive Psychotherapy 12*, 213–230.

Elmore, D.K. and de Castro, J.M. (1990) 'Self-rated moods and hunger in relation to spontaneous eating behaviour in bulimics, recovered bulimics, and normals.' *International Journal of Eating Disorders 9*, 179–190.

Fairburn, C.G. and Cooper, P.J. (1984) 'Binge eating, self induced vomiting and laxative abuse: A community study.' *Psychological Medicine 14*, 401–410.

Fairburn, C.G. and Cooper, P.J. (1989) 'Eating disorders.' In K. Hawton, P.M. Salkovskis, J.Kirk and D.M. Clark (eds) *Cognitive Behaviour Therapy for Psychiatric Problems*. Oxford: Oxford University Press.

Fairburn, C.G., Cooper, Z. and Cooper, P.J. (1986) 'The clinical features and maintenance of bulimia nervosa.' In K.D. Brownell and J.P. Foreyt (eds) *Physiology, Psychology and Treatment of the Eating Disorders*. New York: Basic Books.

Garner, D.M. and Bemis, K.M. (1982) 'A cognitive-behavioural approach to anorexia nervosa.' *Cognitive Therapy and Research 6*, 123–150.

Garner D.M. and Garfinkel, P.E. (1979) 'The Eating Attitudes Test: an index of the symptoms of anorexia nervosa.' *Psychological Medicine 9*, 273–279.

Geller, J., Johnston, C. and Madston, K. (1997) 'The role of shape and weight in self-concept: the shape and weight based self-esteem inventory.' *Cognitive Therapy and Research 21*, 5–24.

Guidano, V.F. and Liotti, G. (1983) *Cognitive Processes and Emotional Disorders*. New York: Guilford Press.

Herman, C.P. and Mack, D. (1975) 'Restrained and unrestrained eating.' *Journal of Personality 43*, 647–660.

Hohlstein, L.A., Smith, G.T. and Atlas, J.G. (1998) 'An application of expectancy theory to eating disorders: development and validation of measures of eating and dieting expectancies.' *Psychological Assessment 10*, 49–58.

Hsu, L.K.G. (1990) 'Experiential aspects of bulimia nervosa.' *Behaviour Modification 14*, 50–65.

Jones, R., Peveler, R.C., Hope, R.A. and Fairburn, C.G. (1993) 'Changes during treatment for bulimia nervosa: a comparison of three psychological treatments.' *Behaviour Research and Therapy 31*, 479–485.

Kaye, W.H., Gwirtsman, H.E., George, D.T., Weiss, S.R. and Jimerson, D.C. (1986) 'Relationship of mood alterations to bingeing behaviour in bulimia.' *British Journal of Psychiatry 149*, 479–485.

Lacey, J.H. (1984) The bulimic syndrome. In A.Ferguson (ed.) *Advanced Medicine*. London: Royal College of Physicians.

Lowe, M.R. Gleaves, D.H., DiSimone-Weiss, R.T., Furgueson, C., Gayda, C.A., Kolsky, P.A., Neal-Walden, T., Nelsen, L.A. and McKinney, S. (1996). 'Restraint, dieting, and the continuum model of bulimia nervosa.' *Journal of Abnormal Psychology 105*, 508–517.

Lowe, M.R., Gleaves, D.H. and Murphy-Eberenz, K.P. (1998) 'On the relation of dieting and bingeing in bulimia nervosa.' *Journal of Abnormal Psychology 107*, 263–271.

Padesky, C.A. and Mooney, K (1995) 'Cognitive therapy of personality disorders: schema change processes.' Paper presented at the European Congress of Behaviour and Cognitive Therapy, London, September.

Phelan, P.W. (1987) 'Cognitive correlates of bulimia: the Bulimic Thoughts Questionnaire.' *International Journal of Eating Disorders 6*, 593–607.

Pinel, J.P.J. (2000) *Biopsychology*. Needham Heights, MA: Allyn and Bacon.

Rorty, M., Yager, J. and Possotto, E. (1994) 'Childhood sexual, physical, and psychological abuse in bulimia nervosa.' *American Journal of Psychiatry 151*, 1122–1126.

Steiger, H., Lehoux, P.M. and Gauvin, L. (1999) 'Impulsivity, dietary control and the urge to binge in bulimic syndromes.' *International Journal of Eating Disorders 26*, 261–274.

Stice, E. and Agras, W.S. (1996) 'Predicting onset and cessation of bulimic behaviours during adolescence: a longitudinal grouping analysis.' *Behaviour Therapy 29*, 257–276.

Stice, E., Nemeroff, C. and Shaw, H. (1996) 'A test of the dual pathway model of bulimia nervosa: Evidence for restrained-eating and affect regulation mechanisms.' *Journal of Social and Clinical Psychology, 15*, 340–363.

Vitousek, K. and Hollon, S.D. (1990) 'The investigation of schematic content and processing in eating disorders.' *Cognitive Therapy and Research 14*, 191–214.

Welch, S.L. and Fairburn, C.G. (1994) 'Sexual abuse and bulimia nervosa: three integrated case control comparisons.' *American Journal of Psychiatry 151*, 402–407.

Wells, A. (1997) *Cognitive Therapy of Anxiety Disorders*. Chichester: Wiley.

Young, J.E. (1990) *Cognitive Therapy for Personality Disorders: A Schema Focussed Approach*. Sarasota: Professional Resource Exchange.

Subject Index

Author Index